PU
BATTLE

After six years of constant bombardment from the forces of the mighty Lizard Man Empire, your beloved city of Vymorna lies in ruins, yet its battered and war-weary troops still hold out. Fighting alongside your mother, Queen Perriel, you know the situation is desperate. It is surely a matter of time before the city must fall into the hands of evil . . . unless the divine powers come to its aid.

Then the great Lord Telak, god of courage, appears in a dream. YOU are the one chosen to carry out the mission to bring victory to your people. Only YOU can seek out the weapon which will aid you and your city against the dark forces. Your mission will take you through enemy lines and will be fraught with danger but you must succeed. YOU are Vymorna's last chance . . .

Two dice, a pencil and an eraser are all you need to embark on this thrilling adventure, which is complete with its elaborate combat system and a score sheet to record your gains and losses.

Many dangers lie ahead and your success is by no means certain. YOU decide which routes to follow, which dangers to risk and which adversaries to fight!

Fighting Fantasy Gamebooks

THE WARLOCK OF FIRETOP MOUNTAIN
THE CITADEL OF CHAOS
THE FOREST OF DOOM
STARSHIP TRAVELLER
CITY OF THIEVES
DEATHTRAP DUNGEON
ISLAND OF THE LIZARD KING
SCORPION SWAMP
CAVERNS OF THE SNOW WITCH
HOUSE OF HELL
TALISMAN OF DEATH
SPACE ASSASSIN
FREEWAY FIGHTER
TEMPLE OF TERROR
THE RINGS OF KETHER
SEAS OF BLOOD
APPOINTMENT WITH F.E.A.R.
REBEL PLANET
DEMONS OF THE DEEP
SWORD OF THE SAMURAI
TRIAL OF CHAMPIONS
ROBOT COMMANDO
MASKS OF MAYHEM
CREATURE OF HAVOC
BENEATH NIGHTMARE CASTLE
CRYPT OF THE SORCERER
STAR STRIDER
PHANTOMS OF FEAR
MIDNIGHT ROGUE
CHASMS OF MALICE
BATTLEBLADE WARRIOR
SLAVES OF THE ABYSS
SKY LORD
STEALER OF SOULS
DAGGERS OF DARKNESS
ARMIES OF DEATH
PORTAL OF EVIL
VAULT OF THE VAMPIRE
FANGS OF FURY
DEAD OF NIGHT

Steve Jackson's *Sorcery!*

1. The Shamutanti Hills
2. Kharé – Cityport of Traps
3. The Seven Serpents
4. The Crown of Kings

FIGHTING FANTASY – The Introductory Role-playing Game
THE RIDDLING REAVER – Four thrilling adventures
OUT OF THE PIT – Fighting Fantasy Monsters
TITAN – The Fighting Fantasy World

Steve Jackson and Ian Livingstone present:

BATTLEBLADE WARRIOR

by Marc Gascoigne

Illustrated by Alan Langford

Puffin Books

PUFFIN BOOKS

Published by the Penguin Group
27 Wrights Lane, London w8 5TZ, England
Viking Penguin Inc., 40 West 23rd Street, New York, New York 10010, USA
Penguin Books Australia Ltd, Ringwood, Victoria, Australia
Penguin Books Canada Ltd, 2801 John Street, Markham, Ontario, Canada L3R 1B4
Penguin Books (NZ) Ltd, 182–190 Wairau Road, Auckland 10, New Zealand

Penguin Books Ltd, Registered Offices: Harmondsworth, Middlesex, England

First published 1988
5 7 9 10 8 6 4

Concept copyright © Steve Jackson and Ian Livingstone, 1988
Text copyright © Marc Gascoigne, 1988
Illustrations copyright © David Gallagher, 1988
All rights reserved

Printed and bound in Great Britain by
Cox & Wyman Ltd, Reading
Filmset in Linotron Palatino by
Rowland Phototypesetting Ltd
Bury St Edmunds, Suffolk

Except in the United States of America,
this book is sold subject to the condition
that it shall not, by way of trade or otherwise,
be lent, re-sold, hired out, or otherwise circulated
without the publisher's prior consent in any form of
binding or cover other than that in which it is
published and without a similar condition
including this condition being imposed
on the subsequent purchaser

*For Bob N., Maggie S., Kevin W. and Stephen K.,
and all the staff at Greylight Industries plc,
for all the fun they're giving me.*

CONTENTS

YOUR CHARACTER
9

HINTS ON PLAY
16

ADVENTURE SHEET
18

VYMORNA BESIEGED!
21

BATTLEBLADE WARRIOR
27

YOUR CHARACTER

You are about to embark on a momentous quest that will decide the fate of not just yourself but a whole city, and possibly an entire country. Before embarking on your great adventure, you must first determine your own strengths and weaknesses. Use dice to discover your *Initial* scores. On pages 18–19 there is an *Adventure Sheet* which you may use to record the details of an adventure. On it you will find boxes for recording your SKILL, STAMINA and LUCK scores.

You are advised either to record your scores on the *Adventure Sheet* in pencil, or to make photocopies of the sheet for use in future adventures.

Skill, Stamina and Luck

Roll one die. Add 6 to this number and enter this total in the SKILL box on the *Adventure Sheet*.

Roll two dice. Add 12 to the number rolled and enter this total in the STAMINA box.

There is also a LUCK box. Roll one die, add 6 to this number and enter this total in the LUCK box.

For reasons that will be explained below, SKILL, STAMINA and LUCK scores change constantly during an adventure. You must keep an accurate record of these scores and for this reason you are advised either to write small in the boxes, or to keep an eraser handy. But never rub out your *Initial* scores.

Although you may be awarded additional SKILL, STAMINA and LUCK points, these totals may never exceed your *Initial* scores, except on very rare occasions, when you will be instructed on a particular page.

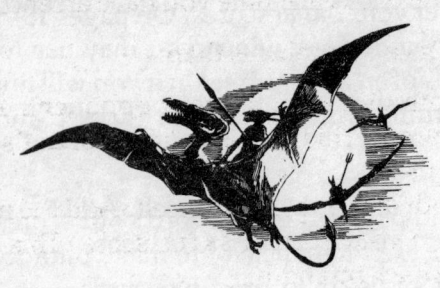

Your SKILL score reflects your swordsmanship and general fighting expertise; the higher the better. Your STAMINA score reflects your general constitution, your will to survive, your determination and your overall fitness; the higher your STAMINA score, the longer you will be able to survive. Your LUCK score indicates how naturally lucky a person you are; it may only be through good luck that you survive! Luck – and magic – are facts of life in the war-torn lands of Southern Allansia through which you will soon be travelling.

Battles

You will often come across pages in the book which instruct you to fight an opponent of some sort. An option to flee may be given, but if not – or if you choose to attack the opponent anyway – you must resolve the battle as described below.

First record your opponent's SKILL and STAMINA scores in the first vacant Encounter Box on your *Adventure Sheet*. The scores for each opponent are given in the book each time you have an encounter.

The sequence of combat is then:

1. Roll both dice once for your opponent. Add its SKILL score. This total is your opponent's Attack Strength.
2. Roll both dice once for yourself. Add the number rolled to your current SKILL score. This total is your Attack Strength.
3. If your Attack Strength is higher than that of your opponent, you have wounded it: proceed to step 4. If your opponent's Attack Strength is higher than yours, it has wounded you: proceed to step 5. If both Attack Strength totals are the same, you have avoided each other's blows – start the next Attack Round from step 1 above.

4. You have wounded your opponent, so subtract 2 points from its STAMINA score. You may use your LUCK here to do additional damage (see over).
5. Your opponent has wounded you, so subtract 2 points from your own STAMINA score. Again you may use LUCK at this stage (see over).
6. Make the appropriate adjustments to either your opponent's or your own STAMINA score (and your LUCK score if you used LUCK – see over).
7. Begin the next Attack Round by returning to your current SKILL score and repeating steps 1–6. This sequence continues until the STAMINA score of either you or your opponent has been reduced to zero (death).

Fighting More Than One Opponent

If you are involved in a fight with more than one opponent, at the start of each Attack Round you must decide which single opponent to attack. After choosing one, roll both dice to determine the Attack

Strength of all the combatants individually. Resolve your own attack against your chosen opponent as usual. Next, compare your current Attack Strength with those of *all* your other opponents except the one you've just fought. Any opponent with a *higher* Attack Strength than yours will score a hit against you, with the usual loss of 2 STAMINA points. Remember: you can score hits *only* against the opponent you chose at the start of the round.

Luck

At various times during your adventure, either in battles or when you come across situations in which you could either be Lucky or Unlucky (details of these are given on the pages themselves), you may call on your LUCK to make the outcome more favourable. But beware! Using LUCK is a risky business and if you are *Un*lucky, the results could be disastrous.

The procedure for using your LUCK is as follows: roll two dice. If the number rolled is equal to or less than your current LUCK score, you have been Lucky and the result will go in your favour. If the number rolled is higher than your current LUCK score, you have been Unlucky and you will be penalized.

This procedure is known as *Testing your Luck*. Each time you *Test your Luck*, you must subtract 1 point from your current LUCK score. Thus you will soon realize that the more you rely on your LUCK, the more risky this will become.

Using Luck in Battles

On certain pages of the book you will be told to *Test your Luck* and will be told the consequences of your being Lucky or Unlucky. However, in battles you always have the option of using your LUCK either to inflict a more serious wound on an opponent you have just wounded, or to minimize the effects of a wound your opponent has just inflicted on you!

If you have just wounded the opponent, you may *Test your Luck* as described above. If you are Lucky you have inflicted a severe wound and may subtract an extra 2 points from the opponent's STAMINA score. However, if you are Unlucky the wound was a mere graze and you must restore 1 point to your opponent's STAMINA (i.e. instead of scoring the normal 2 points of damage you have now scored only 1).

If your opponent has just wounded you, you may *Test your Luck* to try to minimize the wound. If you are Lucky you have managed to avoid the full

damage of the blow. Restore 1 point of STAMINA (i.e. instead of doing 2 points of damage it has done only 1). If you are Unlucky, you have taken a more serious blow. Subtract 1 extra STAMINA point.

Remember that you must subtract 1 point from your own LUCK score each time you *Test your Luck*.

HINTS ON PLAY

Skill

As you are already a battle-hardened warrior with many fights behind you in defence of your besieged city, your SKILL score is above average. It will not change much during your adventure, and you may only change it if specifically instructed. As SKILL is a measure of combat prowess, it can be reduced, for instance by losing your weapon or by the effects of something like poison. Acquiring an enchanted weapon could increase your SKILL – but remember that you can only use one weapon at a time.

Stamina

Your STAMINA will change more frequently as your journey continues, as you suffer wounds and exhaustion and then, hopefully, recover. At various times you will be given opportunities to eat some of the supplies you carry with you. Eating 1 Provision restores up to 4 STAMINA points; you may eat only 1 Provision at a time, even though you may have more (you can carry up to 4 Provisions at any one time). Your STAMINA may never exceed its *Initial* value.

Luck

The eyes of the gods are upon you in your quest. Your patrons will attempt to help you, but their rivals will set deadly enemies and traps in your path to thwart their plans. You will need to use your LUCK wisely and sparingly if you are to survive and vanquish the forces of Evil. There may be occasions when your LUCK will improve and you can recover some points, but the score may never exceed its *Initial* value.

Getting Started

Read the introductory tale, which begins on page 21, then turn to paragraph 1. It is recommended that you make notes and draw a map as you travel. There *is* a way of successfully completing the quest that involves only minimal risk of failure or death, but you will need all your SKILL – and LUCK – to find it. Be warned: the object of your quest is never fully revealed to you, so to be successful you must make use of the clues presented to you to deduce just what it is you need to find.

ADVENTURE SHEET

SKILL *Initial Skill =*	STAMINA *Initial Stamina =*	LUCK *Initial Luck =*

ITEMS OF EQUIPMENT CARRIED

SPECIAL ITEMS

Bow and ← ← ← arows

PROVISIONS REMAINING

MONSTER ENCOUNTER BOXES

Skill = *Stamina* =	*Skill* = *Stamina* =	*Skill* = *Stamina* =
Skill = *Stamina* =	*Skill* = *Stamina* =	*Skill* = *Stamina* =
Skill = *Stamina* =	*Skill* = *Stamina* =	*Skill* = *Stamina* =
Skill = *Stamina* =	*Skill* = *Stamina* =	*Skill* = *Stamina* =

VYMORNA BESIEGED!

As the might of the Lizard Man Empire smashed like an ocean breaker against its walls once more, the besieged city of Vymorna shuddered – but held. Along the ragged lines of its shattered walls desperate men and women fought, though they were dying on their feet. Their energy sapped by six years of starvation and malnutrition, the battered troops held firm through sheer will-power. For every pace the reptilian troops gained, the defenders vowed a hundred lizard corpses would lie. But the Lizard Men could bear such losses, and more, for the might of the Lizard King's armies was colossal. Soon, very soon, the evil humanoids would break Vymorna's last ring of defences, even if they had to dismantle the city stone by stone, brick by brick. The Empire of the Lizard Kings would not rest until all the lands of Southern Allansia were ensnared under its cruel dominion.

Inside the City

All this you know, for your mother is Queen Perriel, the lion-hearted woman who now commands Vymorna's defences. Your father, Alexandros the Second, was struck down by a poisoned javelin in a counter-attack to keep the reptilian hordes from the outer wall of the castle at the centre of the city. His death made a warrior of your mother, but this, and years of constant bombardment, has changed her beyond belief. Where once she was beauty and grace, she is now thin-lipped sternness, her eyes red-ringed through lack of sleep and the side-effects of her sorcerous searches for supernatural aid. Night after night the Queen pleads with the gods and their servants for divine help against the overwhelming odds, and each night she receives no answer. It is as if there is a war in the heavens as well as on Titan, and the forces of Evil and Chaos are winning there, too.

Your father's death also made a warrior of you, and now you ride into battle alongside your mother. Between raids and wall duties you help tend the sick, arrayed in rows in the Great Hall of the castle. There are wounded warriors by the score, but also a great many women and children, injured by flying missiles or simply suffering from malnutrition. Food is now very scarce and strictly rationed, and it is only owing to good planning that it has lasted so long.

Troubled Dreams

What is perhaps worse than the lack of food is the constant lack of sleep. It would be hard enough to sleep, anyway, with the bombardment of rocks and exploding balls of sulphur, but each night the enemy conjure up spirits and demons, which howl around the towers of the castle until dawn. Their screaming, often joined by sorcerous thunder and lightning, would keep all but the most desperately tired awake.

However on this night even you sleep. You spent most of the evening helping to put out a massive fire blazing in the south tower of the castle, started by a flaming brand, which had hurtled into the city from one of the many giant catapults stationed just out of reach of the city's archers. When the fire was out you didn't bother returning to your quarters in the main keep, but just found an empty corner, pulled your stained cloak over yourself and slept.

Dawn breaks and you awake, savouring the warmth of your corner and the light on your eyes before opening them. But the castle is somehow different. You lie still for a moment, before sitting up with a start. There's nothing but silence! Everywhere is quiet, so quiet you can hear your breath coming in short gulps as you rub the sleep from your eyes with your dirty fists to find yourself alone in a corner of the Inner Hall. All you can see are the bare, rubble-strewn flagstones, the first traces of weeds poking up between them as if stretching for the sunlight, which beams through the gaps in the shattered roof. 'By Telak's golden sword!' you exclaim aloud, using the oath your mother always forbade you to utter in those far-off days before the siege. The siege! you remember. The siege . . . and Mother! What in the name of all the heavens is going on?

*

'Indeed you may ask,' comes a voice from behind you. You spin round and look up in wonder. Atop the ruined wall above you stands a glowing figure, a hefty warrior armed for battle and clad in brilliant golden armour. About his feet stalks a lion, which must be fully grown though it is dwarfed by the radiant figure. 'Know you not who I am, my child? You called on me just a moment ago, though in truth I was here awaiting you,' the warrior intones in a voice that rumbles like thunder round a distant mountain. His gleaming emerald eyes stare deep into yours, flashing with supernatural power.

The Task of Telak

You drop to your knees, more out of amazement than respect, for you know now that the figure before you is Telak, the Swordbearer, Lord of Courage and patron of all who bear arms against Evil. 'My lord,' you stammer, 'what would you have of me?'

'Do not be afraid,' rumbles the heavenly voice, 'for you must listen carefully to what I tell you. The dark forces that oppose both of us are gathering for a final assault. Even as I speak, demonic legions begin to batter at the gates of my ethereal palace, just as they batter at the very doors of yours. What is needed is an Earthly victory against Evil, and soon, to divert the Lizard King's deathless masters away from my door so I can properly come to Vymorna's aid.

'Know you of a place called the Durtelakin, Telak's

Mount? It is one of twin peaks in the Lion Heights, far to the north-east of Vymorna. You must go there and find a weapon which will aid you and your city against Evil. Seek out the man they call Laskar.' The golden warrior's voice fades, as if his attention were elsewhere, and the lion at his legs growls. 'I must depart to secure my own gates. Go, and serve me well. Wheresoever I can I will aid you, for you are a warrior now, and under my protection.'

The golden warrior and his lion fade away . . . and a rough hand is shaking you awake. Through the musty gloom of the Inner Hall you can see others rising and shaking themselves. From all around you comes the sound of coughing, stamping, chattering, mingled with the distant sounds of battle.

The Mission

'It is decided, then. All the omens are with you. You must depart as soon as you are able.' Your mother looks stern, but you know from her eyes that she is dreading your leaving on such a dangerous mission. Around the room, everyone shares Queen Perriel's mingled look of trepidation and resolve, but all nod their heads at the decision. 'You will leave a few hours before dawn, to give you the best chance of crossing through the enemy's encampment. In the darkness you may be able to pass through their lines, though I still fear for you.'

'I was chosen, Mother,' you state simply, and leave to prepare for your journey. Turn to **1**.

1

Dawn is not far away. All night the bombardment of the city has continued, but somehow you managed to rest and relax a little in preparation for your journey. Now, with the moon set and the first few glimmers of light on the horizon, you are in the secluded room of your mother, Queen Perriel, making your final preparations for your journey. You are dressed in sturdy clothes, but with minimal armour so you can move quickly. You have a strong cloak to protect you from the elements and to keep you warm at night. There is a large rucksack filled with supplies (4 Provisions), and your trusty sword and hunting-knife.

While you are getting ready, the Queen goes to a chest and pulls three items from it. 'These belonged to your father,' she says, 'and I know he would want them to be put to good use.' You may take two of the objects by going to the appropriate paragraphs; make a note of those you choose on your *Adventure Sheet*. There are a bow and three silvered arrows (turn to **13**), a bottle containing a pale liquid (turn to **388**), and a small glass globe filled with a swirling cloud of dust specks (turn to **31**).

2

At the bottom of the steps, you have arrived in another old and very dusty room, littered again with small pieces of rubble from its cracked ceiling and walls. In a far corner what may be a statue or perhaps a fountain casts grotesque shadows in the lantern-light. Do you take one of the dark passages that lead off to the left (turn to **255**) and to the right (turn to **271**), or do you examine the statue or fountain (turn to **35**)?

3

Your hunting-knife slashes out and cuts away part of the web. Pulling yourself upright, you are faced by the Wasp Spider. You have no time to find your sword, and must defend yourself with your knife.

WASP SPIDER   SKILL 6   STAMINA 2

If the Wasp Spider scores a hit against you, do not deduct the normal 2 STAMINA points. Instead, roll one die and lose as many STAMINA points as the result of your roll. The bite of the Wasp Spider is highly poisonous! If you succeed in beating the venomous Spider, turn to **356**.

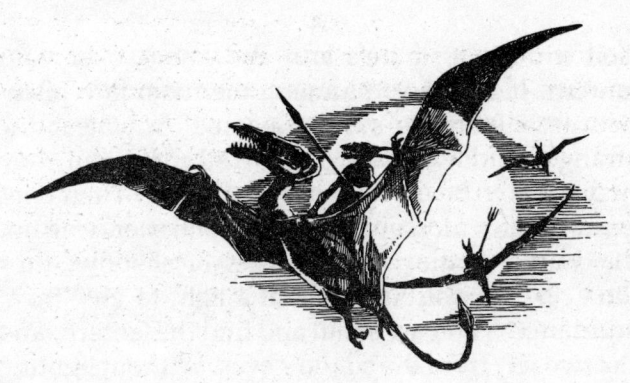

4

You walk to the top of the stairs and peer down. They seem very steep, and it is very dark down there. Then you draw back hurriedly, for you are sure you heard voices down there. Yes, there they are again: Lizard Men! You run for the other steps and leap up them quickly, hearing the clatter of the enemy's boots on the flagstones in the distance behind you. You come to a door, and once you have gone through, it slams shut behind you. In alarm you notice there is no lock, and gazing around you realize there is nothing to bar it with either. In blind terror you race down the corridor, pausing only long enough to notice that it is lined on either side by barred cells, until you reach another door at the far end. You kick at it – and it holds firm. It's locked! Your heart sinks. Will you continue trying to force it (turn to **321**) or look for a key (turn to **264**)?

5

You trip on a statue's arm and knock over your lantern. It goes out, plunging the room into pitch-darkness. You are surely doomed! You hear the strange shadow-creatures howl near by, but then they seem to be moving away from you. Their cries grow quieter until you are left in total silence again. Of course! If they are creatures of shadow, they won't be very strong without a light to give them substance! You paw about and find the lantern, and the two jets from the statue's eyes. Without lighting the lantern, you creep across the room, hoping that the Shadow Ghouls have definitely gone. You reach the far passage and head up it. When you feel you have put enough distance between yourself and the room you pause to calm your ragged nerves, and to light your lantern. You are alone; add 1 LUCK point. Walking on, you come to a new set of stairs, twisted and crumbling, which lead down. Turn to **152**.

6

A horrendous grinding, crashing sound rends the air as your boat is torn in two. A split second before it is engulfed you dive into the water. Holding your breath, you try to swim away to surface safely, but the water is very turbulent as the galley sails above you. A great oar sweeps towards you, knocking the air from your lungs. Immediately you're gulping water and choking . . . drowning . . . dead.

7

Your tortured imagination can bear it no longer. Your nerve snaps and you turn and flee into the mist, but the voices and faces are all around you. You clutch your head and scream but no sound comes out. Dead faces loom out of the mist; swords and axes wielded by skeletal hands scythe the air around you. You fall to your knees in sheer terror. The roar of battle is all around. Metal clashes on metal and bone; screams and curses howl in your ears. The grinning death's-head faces of warriors long dead close in around you. Soon you will join their legion. Your quest is at an end.

8

You barge into the nearest tent, and are stopped in your tracks by a very rupulsive sight! A Lizard Woman is reclining in her tent amid the myriad smells emanating from the burning incense pots, the luxurious slime bath and her own foul body. You are quite overpowered, but you know you must do something before she can react. Will you turn and run from the tent (turn to 319), say something (turn to 254) or attack her (turn to 149)?

9

The following morning you rise with the dawn, feeling more refreshed and relaxed than you have in a very long while. Thoughts of the journey still ahead linger, though, and so it is with a sad smile that you bid farewell to White-eye and plunge into the thick jungle, hacking a path with your knife. The sun is soon high and it becomes desperately hot. The sweat drips from you as you slowly carve a path through the tangled undergrowth. By noon you have made good headway. As you travel you pick up more Provisions (up to the maximum of 4). After another hour or so you stop in the shade of a large tree and eat (deduct 1 Provision and recover STAMINA as usual). Suitably refreshed, you press on. Turn to 94.

10

An enormous green-skinned Hobgoblin leaps at you from the mêlée. Rabid and foaming at the mouth with blood-lust brought on by the battle, the foul creature yells a war-cry and swings his huge nail-studded mace at you!

HOBGOBLIN
   FANATIC   SKILL 7   STAMINA 6

If it scores two consecutive hits against you, turn to **306**. If you score two consecutive hits, or kill the Hobgoblin, roll a die. If you roll 1–2, turn to **322**; 3–4, turn to **187**; 5–6, turn to **192**.

11

You tell White-eye the whole story, leaving out nothing. He frowns with anxiety as he hears of the siege, looks deeply interested in the account of your dream, and seems at times thrilled and horrified by the tale of your quest so far. You feel comfortable here, and talk far into the night. Your narrative is disturbed by animal howls from outside the caravan, but the old man calms you. 'Don't fret: friends protect us. We cannot be harmed here.' You resume your tale. When it is finally at an end, White-eye leans forward in his chair and says, 'I have some news regarding this Laskar whom you seek. I do not give freely, but I will gladly trade with you.' You cannot trade your father's things, but you may have something else to exchange. What can you trade?

Black lotus essence	Turn to **249**
Cloth o' gold	Turn to **49**
A mace	Turn to **129**
An Orc charm	Turn to **256**
A phial of purple liquid	Turn to **344**
A small panther idol	Turn to **389**

If you have nothing, or if you do not wish to trade, turn to **111**.

12

You steer your small boat for mid-stream. The sun is already making the air humid, and a thin haze of steamy mist sits on the cooler water. You could avoid the mist by steering for the north shore (turn to **295**) or continue in mid-stream (turn to **60**).

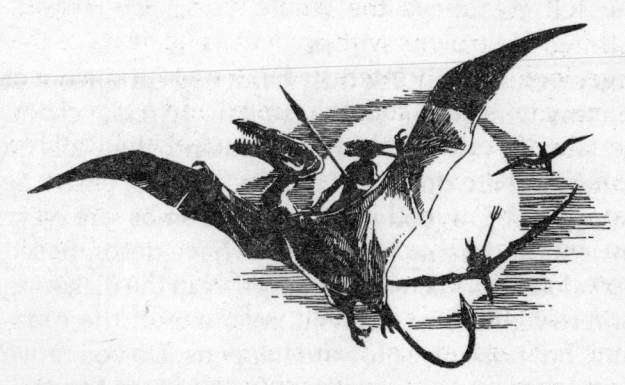

13

The bow is made from finely worked bone, and has a great many charms and sigils carved into it. Its three silvered arrows are turned to perfection, and you know that whenever you fire one you will be almost guaranteed of hitting and destroying your target. (Note down the bow and three arrows on your *Adventure Sheet*; every time you use an arrow you must cross it off.) If you have another item to choose, turn to **31** for the swirling globe or turn to **388** for the phial of liquid. If you now have your two items, turn to **361**.

14

You carefully push the dust-hardened curtain out of the way with your sword, revealing a circular chamber with an exit on its far wall. Cut into the walls on either side are dozens of narrow shelves, each one occupied by a body. These catacombs are very ancient, and many of the bodies have decomposed to skeletons, which look quite grisly in the flickering lantern-light. Gingerly you poke one of the cadavers, but nothing untoward happens. Do you move on (turn to **297**) or investigate further (turn to **351**)?

15

Did you think that creatures such as these would bow down in servitude to a priest of Telak? These are the servants of Chaos! Turn to **70**.

16

An incredibly hot sheet of flame explodes upwards into the sky, carrying with it the screams of dying Lizard Men. You turn away disgusted: surely it isn't right to fight in such a way? Lecarte, it seems, has no qualms – he's leaping up and down, cheering and yelling, with Snag capering round him. Leading Lecarte's horse by the reins, you set off on foot for Capra. Turn to **89**.

17

Covered by your cloak, you lie in the soft undergrowth and wait for sleep to come. The moon rises between the trees as you lie listening to the croaks, whistles and chirps of the jungle's nocturnal inhabitants until you fall asleep. Turn to **219**.

18

You scurry along the trench, keeping your head down to avoid being spotted. Suddenly you hear a loud, brash laugh from above you. You peer up, to see a huge Two-headed Lizard Man looking down at you from the side of the trench, brandishing a long, curving sword. There's no chance to use your bow, if you have it. You can leap out and attack him (turn to **30**), or grab his foot and try to pull him down into the trench (turn to **62**).

19

You land with a bump a moment later and your lantern goes out. You reach out for it and recoil! You touched something scaly that wriggled under your hand! Leaping back flat against the wall, you find your lantern again, and hastily light it. Oh, Telak! Snakes – black, viper-like snakes. Your mind races in panic as your horrified eyes scan the room. There is a large pile of rags and rubbish in the corner nearest you, and a passage leading off from the wall opposite you. Will you try to reach the exit (turn to **179**) or the rags (turn to **110**)?

20

The Krell you are chasing drops your sword and scampers off, swinging up into the branches with dextrous ease. It swings there, chattering and screaming, mocking you in a playful fashion. You retrieve your sword, gather up your things and move on. Turn to **221**.

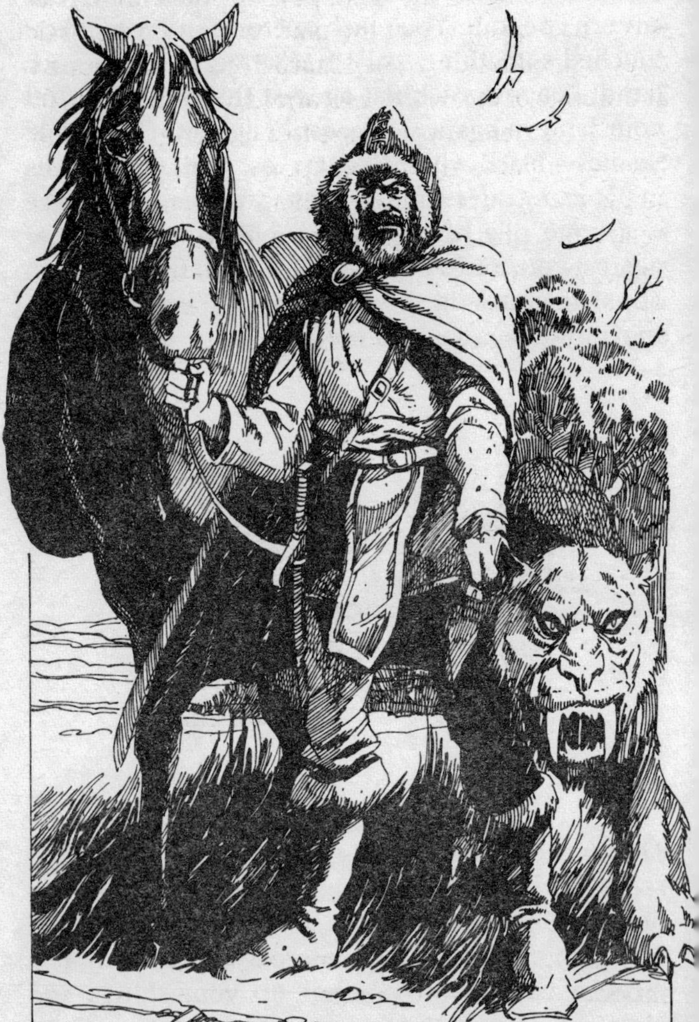

21

'Come on!' shouts the man, pulling you with him as if you had no choice in the matter. You glance back over your shoulder. The Lizard Men have stopped at the edge of the copse, as if afraid to venture into it. A little further in, you come to a clearing. Tethered here are a horse and a small pony, both apparently grazing. As you approach them the pony lifts its head and you halt. It is not a pony at all but a Sabre-toothed Tiger! 'Easy, Snag,' says the stranger. 'Look, fresh lizard!' If you have your father's bow, turn to **284**; otherwise, turn to **98**.

22

You hail the travellers, greeting them cordially. There is no reply: they sit motionless on their mounts, who regard you with cold, lizard eyes. A chill breeze springs up, and you give a quick shudder. 'What's the matter? Have you lost your tongues?' you cry. Turn to **247**.

23

Through sheer momentum you have bludgeoned a way through the enemy lines, and many of your fellow warriors are with you. Pausing only to slash stray Swamp Goblins and panicked Lizard Men out of your way, you race on. A frightened riding lizard skitters across your path and you manage to grab its bridle and stop it. The enemy are regrouping behind you. If you are to escape you must go now. Do you want to try to ride the lizard (turn to **59**) or escape on foot (turn to **144**)?

24

They seem to be waiting, too, sitting motionless on their steeds. The peculiar lizards look at you both with cold, emotionless eyes. You shudder, and Katya does, too, as a chill of foreboding grips your body. And then, without a word or sign from their riders, the lizards start to move slowly towards you. Turn to **247**.

25

Gathering all your strength, you give a sudden surge and burst from the web. In its anger the Wasp Spider stings you as you jump up, knocking it flying into the undergrowth. Roll one die: deduct as many STAMINA points as the result of the roll – the bite of the Wasp Spider is highly poisonous and often deadly. If you survive the sting you rest awhile, before staggering in the direction of the river to wash and refresh yourself. Turn to **356**.

26

The massive Lizard Man Champion looks down at you from his bloodied perch, sneers an ugly sneer, and leaps to join battle with you. He is using his giant axe as his main weapon, but also attacks with a huge pointed dagger (treat it as a second opponent with the same SKILL value as the axe – if you lose to it, you take damage; otherwise you hold it off).

LIZARD MAN
  CHAMPION   SKILL 12   STAMINA 18

If he scores three hits against you, turn to **96**. If by some good fortune you defeat, or kill, the Champion, turn to **166**.

27

Keeping the dark, forbidding tangle of the jungle always on your right hand, you decide to head northwards. Away to the west is the southern extent of the Axehead Plain; as you gaze out over it you notice that something is burning on the horizon. Could it be Vymorna? No, it's too far north, you decide; it must be somewhere else under attack. You peer further south but cannot pick out the city from the haze. Will you keep heading north (turn to **331**), or change your mind and head directly east (turn to **175**)?

28

Howling for vengeance for his treachery you leap at Laskar. The old man looks momentarily frightened, but parries your blow easily, knocking you aside. The Lizard Men surround you, their swords raised for the final blows, which you know must come. Your adventure is over.

29

You run down the rough-walled passage before emerging in a much wider, very dusty tunnel that leads off both to the left and to the right. After some consideration you choose to go right and follow the passage as it leads down a shallow slope and into a large room. The room is empty of life, but features a row of large stone slabs that look (from the red patches splattered on them) as if they were used for dissecting bodies or some similarly gruesome activity. Around the walls lie the shards of smashed pots and vases, but most seem to be filled with ashes – you dare not think of what! Passages lead off straight ahead (turn to 357) and to the left (turn to 385).

30

The Lizard Man swings his sword at you as you clamber out of the trench, scoring an instant hit (deduct 2 STAMINA points).

TWO-HEADED
  LIZARD MAN   SKILL 9   STAMINA 8

If you defeat him, you may sneak away among the tents of the Lizard Man camp (turn to 294).

31

The globe contains fragments of crystal from petrified glow-worms. All you need do is shake the globe, which will light up, slowly fading after about five minutes. If you have another item to choose, turn to **388** for the phial of liquid, or turn to **13** for the bow and arrows. If you already have two items, turn to **361**.

32

The ruins turn into those of the ancient docks of Vymorna. All around you are warehouses and boatyards, once bustling with trade, now shattered and empty. You move on. Will you keep to the alleyways (turn to **203**), or sneak through the warehouse ruins (turn to **261**)?

33

There is no sign of anyone who might have built the platform, nor any indication of why it should be here at all. A rickety rope-bridge overgrown with vines and creepers leads off between the trees to another platform a fair distance away. You are steeling yourself to cross it when you notice a knotted creeper hanging down from higher up one of the immense trees. Will you take the bridge (turn to **199**) or climb the rope (turn to **243**)?

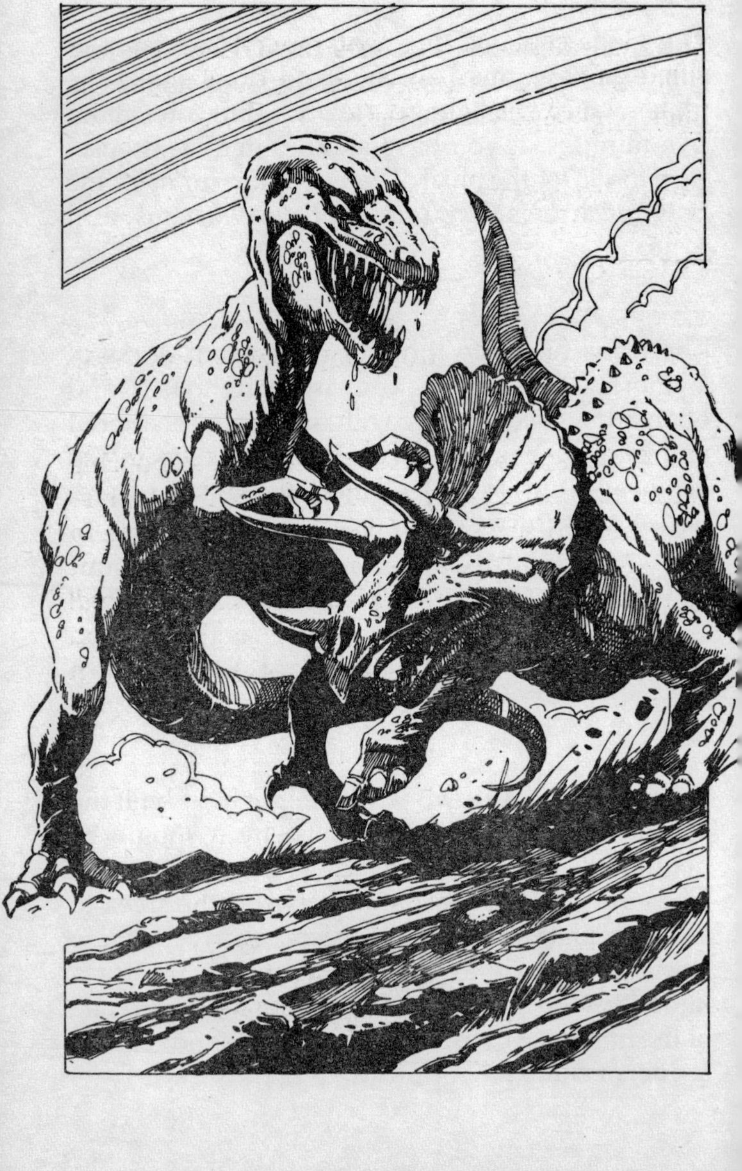

34

The Tyrannosaurus Rex sees the Triceratops and bellows its rage. Leaping down the slope it grabs its huge opponent and attacks.

		SKILL	STAMINA
TYRANNOSAURUS REX	3 attacks	14	19
TRICERATOPS	2 attacks	12	18

You may fight the battle out if you wish, but by the time it is over you are well away from it. Turn to **76**.

35

It is a fountain, with a small statue of Telak pouring water into a shallow bowl. The water that trickles out, though, seems very dark. You catch some in your hand and examine it in the light of your lantern. Oh, Telak! It isn't water at all – it's *blood*! What evil has poisoned this place? You hurry from the room – you may go left (turn to **255**) or right (turn to **271**).

36

With howls of war-cries and the clash of metal on metal, battle is joined. You should fight it out. The Lizard Men attack in twos, and their opponents are Snag, Lecarte and yourself. The combatants each have the following profile:

		SKILL	STAMINA
LIZARD MEN	each	8	7
LECARTE		11	14
SNAG		12	8

Snag can make two attacks, but only on the same opponent. Any Lizard Men not involved in a fight will attempt to fire arrows into one of the battles. First, determine which battle they are aiming at, then roll one die. If you roll a 1, the arrow hits a Lizard Man; if you roll a 6, the arrow hits you or one of your allies. For each hit, deduct 1 STAMINA point. Eventually the skirmish will be over. If you win you may head for the relative safety of Capra. Turn to **89**.

37

You sneak up to the dozing aviator – and hit him across the head with the flat of your sword! He falls to the floor and lies still. Your troubles aren't over yet, though, as the Pterodactyl saw what happened and has taken fright. It's squawking and screeching fit to bust. Shouts come from the tents behind you. You must escape quickly. Will you leap on to the Pterodactyl and fly out of the camp (turn to **387**)? Or would you rather put your trust in a riding lizard (turn to **146**)?

38

You rest awhile, letting your panic subside and getting your breath back, before moving on. You prise open the door to reveal a short corridor, which leads to yet another door – does this place never end? You creep the length of the corridor and listen at the door, but hear nothing except the sound of gently running water. You force the door and almost slip sideways, for this room is at a very bizarre angle. More importantly, the door opposite you is behind a large gout of dark water, which is flowing through wide cracks in the wall and ceiling. Carefully, trying to avoid the flow, you move to the door. Turn to **82**.

39

Voices and faces surround you, swirling in the mist. You grit your teeth and try to stand firm. The battle rages on. With wide eyes and an ever-increasing sense of terror you stare at the ghostly warriors, all bedecked in ancient armour, their fleshless skulls grinning like death's heads as they fight on. You must do something about this. Will you command these visions to depart in the name of Telak (turn to **299**), in the name of your illustrious ancestors (turn to **232**), or stay where you are and watch (turn to **7**)?

40

Roll two dice. If you roll equal to or below your SKILL score, turn to **339**. If you roll above your SKILL score, turn to **109**.

41

The passageway, strewn with dust and rubble like so much of this underground maze, continues for a while, and then turns to the right. At the corner, though, you stop, for the tunnel ends in a wall of rubble – a dead end. Will you attempt to dig through the wall (turn to **128**), or would you rather retrace your steps and take the exit on the left (turn to **125**), or try the tunnel (turn to **67**)?

42

This healing draught will cure some of your wounds. Each time you take it (you may do so twice), roll one die, add 2 to the number you roll and recover as many STAMINA points. Bear in mind that your STAMINA score may not exceed its *Initial* level. You may take the draught at any time, providing you are not doing something strenuous like fighting or running, and that you are not restrained, tied up or in any way kept from making a normal action. Now return to the paragraph you came from.

43

The huddled shapes stand upright, revealing themselves to be three Rat Man engineers. They squeak a challenge and draw their shortswords. Luckily the trench is so narrow you need fight only one at a time. The first one leaps for you.

	SKILL	STAMINA
First RAT MAN	5	6
Second RAT MAN	6	6
Third RAT MAN	6	5

If you defeat the Rat Men, you may move on to the right (turn to **206**), or to the left (turn to **277**).

44

After your 'visitor', you spend a restless night. You are determined to stay awake until dawn, but you find you keep dropping off to sleep. When you wake again the sun is already climbing in the morning sky. You scramble down from the tree and head off towards the river to wash and refresh yourself. Turn to **356**.

45

Oh, crikey! You clutch your stomach and turn blue, trying to stop the feeling that a rat is gnawing you from the inside! Guursh is deadly! Roll one die and lose as many STAMINA points as the result of your roll. If there is a chance that you're still alive after making such a drastic mistake, turn to **161**.

46

Your kick catches Laskar in the jaw, knocking him flying. You grab for the sword and one of the jewels. Note down which one you choose on your *Adventure Sheet* (you may only choose from those you threw on the floor):

Diamond	Turn to **371**
Emeralds	Turn to **228**
Jets	Turn to **173**
Ruby	Turn to **293**

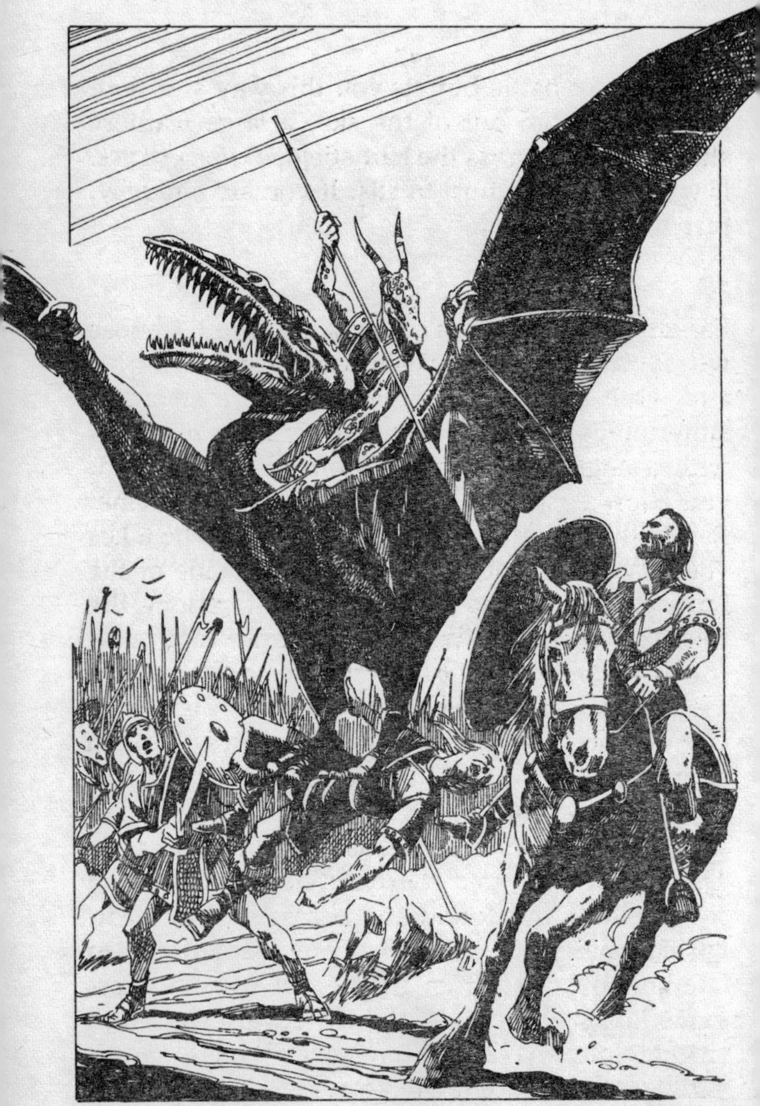

47

The press of battle buffets you this way and that. And then, from out of the sky, a large leathery shape swoops across the battlefield. *Test your Luck*. If you are Lucky, turn to **184**. If you are Unlucky, turn to **147**.

48

Laskar finds all kinds of equipment for you. Choose what you do not already have from the following list and write it on your *Adventure Sheet*: a sword, a lantern plus supply of oil and some flints to light it with, a length of rope, 4 Provisions. Fully equipped, you allow Laskar to lead you back to the ravine. Rather than climbing to the edge, though, he takes you by a wide sloping path down the side of the huge cut. The going is hard, and before long the track is so steep and rocky that you must rope yourselves together. Eventually you reach the base of the ravine and stand looking out across the ruined city with its once-beautiful buildings now lying at strange angles, twisted and cracked by their fall. Laskar leads you through the city, bringing you to where a huge depression leads down into the earth. The roof of a covered courtyard has fallen in, and several dark and forbidding passages lead off it. Laskar points one out. 'That one leads down to another courtyard from where you will find passages leading to the crypts, the royal palace and chief temple. I have not been further than the courtyard.' You embrace the old man and he departs to climb up to the temple on the north side of the ravine and await your successful emergence from the underground complex. Will you descend into the darkness (turn to **289**), or pause awhile (turn to **367**)?

49

White-eye peers at the cloth, picks at it with a long fingernail, rubs it between his palms – then blows his nose on it! You object most strongly, but he calms you, saying that it is just a worthless piece of ordinary cloth dyed a golden colour and shows you the dye that has come off on his hands. Turn to **11** and choose again.

50

It is a fountain, with a small statue of Telak pouring water into a shallow bowl. The water which trickles out now, though, seems very dark. You catch some in your hand and examine it in the light of your lantern. Oh, Telak! It isn't water at all – it's *blood*! What evil has poisoned this place? You hurry from the room. Turn to **271**.

51

All day you wait, swapping nervous stories with Lecarte. Finally, as the sun is setting, the sound of hoofs comes from the west. In addition to those whom you fought earlier, there are six more Lizard Men – quite a force to be taken on by two adventurers and a tiger! The warriors ride up and head straight for the copse. This is it – there is no escape now. Turn to **36**.

52

Roll two dice. If you roll less than or equal to your SKILL score, turn to **180**. If you roll more than your SKILL score, turn to **115**.

53

But you will need more than luck now that you are being chased by half a dozen Lizard Men, all mounted on riding lizards very much like yours. You spur your steed, and race away from the enemy lines. The chase is on! Turn to **177**.

54

You creep between the trees, starting at every rustle. After only a few steps you come to a small grassy clearing, dotted with bushes holding brightly coloured flowers and fruit. Surely this is too good to be true? you think. It simply *must* be a trap! You may wish to enter the clearing (turn to **279**), or perhaps you would rather return to your original path (turn to **257**).

55

Aaaarrghh! Over the edge you go. You land on a large pile of broken floorboards and other trash. Roll one die. If you roll 1–4, you must deduct as many STAMINA points as the result of your roll. If you roll 5–6, you were lucky and avoided injury. After resting down there for a moment, you pull yourself out of the collapsed cellar, and move on. Turn to **32**.

56

You wake up with a jolt and go rigid as all the hairs on the back of your neck stand up. Something large is crawling along the branch towards you, dragging something behind it! You freeze, wishing you could sink back into the tree-trunk against which you are pressed. The thing gets larger, and you can hear the faint rasping of its breath. Will you attack it (turn to **225**), make a light (turn to **143**), or just stay still and hope that somehow it fails to notice you (turn to **352**)?

57

Suddenly there are Lizard Men everywhere, all slashing and cutting with their weapons. You don't stand a chance. Falling to the ground, the precious blood draining from your body, the last thing you hear is Laskar's laughter, an embodiment of pure Evil.

58

Steeling yourself for a trap, you thrust in your hand and grab a small, hard object. Slowly, nervously, you withdraw it, expecting every second something nasty to happen. It's a small idol, carved from some strange metal, depicting a panther-headed god like the larger figures dotted around the overgrown temple. You tuck it away in your rucksack, and press on. Turn to **245**.

59

The riding lizard is jittery, but you are an expert on horseback and the technique seems much the same. You grab the reins and swing yourself up into the small saddle. You kick your legs and with a screech it hares away. Maybe you are not such an expert after all – the Lizard is *very* difficult to control as it gallops about on only two legs! Roll two dice. If you roll higher than your SKILL score, turn to **260**. If you roll less than or equal to your SKILL score, turn to **91**.

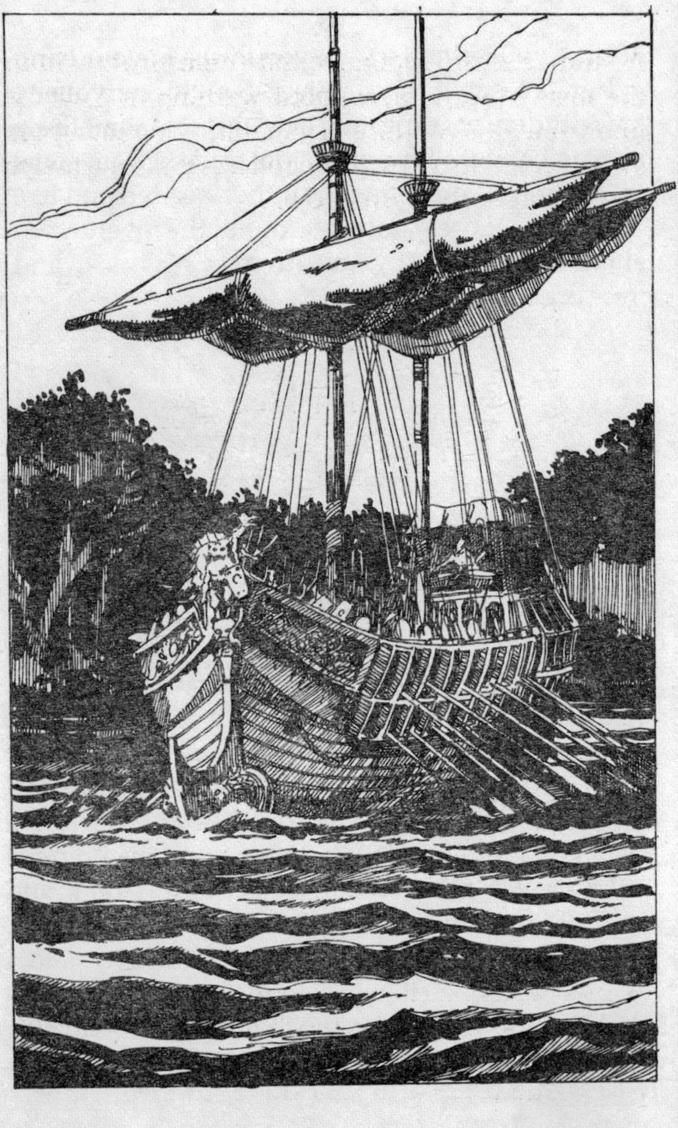

60

A strange, soft lapping sound comes from within the mist. And then, without warning, a galley is upon you! Roll two dice. If you roll higher than your SKILL score, turn to **6**. If you roll less than or equal to your SKILL score, turn to **136**.

61

The rickety caravan is packed to the rafters with an incredible assortment of items. Bats hang from hooks, glass jars full of amazing things line the shelves, strange tapestries are piled thick on the floor. Candles in the corners flicker and dance as if animated, throwing wondrous shadows. The old man speaks: 'Welcome, young one, to the home of White-eye. I am a trader. I deal in anything and everything: advice, rare items from near and far, healing, heart's-ease, food and rest. I give and I receive, a fair exchange. Now, tell me your story and you can stay here for the night . . .' Do you want to tell him (turn to **11**), or would you rather not (turn to **108**)?

62

With a growl the Lizard Man slips over the edge of the trench. A sickening sound follows and his broken body lies still. Luckily for you, he fell on his sword; add 1 LUCK point. You continue along the trench, following it for some way before it ends in a set of rough wooden steps. You clamber up them and peer over the top. Turn to **294**.

63

All at once you are at the clearing. Dark shapes mounted on larger ones mill about in confusion, trapped by your simple barriers. You toss your taper high over their heads and turn and run. As you fly through the trees a vast sheet of flame springs up behind you, mingled with the screams of the dying Lizard Men. At a safe distance you stop and look back, feeling disgusted at what you have done. Always taught to fight fair, you feel you have somehow cheated. Lecarte rides up, all smiles. 'Come, my friend, let's go.' Offering you his big hand he helps you up into the saddle behind him and you set off for Capra, with Snag capering around your mount's legs. Turn to **89**.

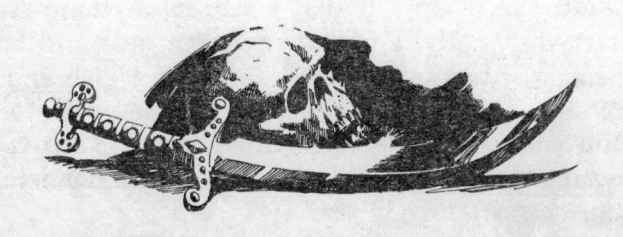

64

You freeze instantly. That last cry was too artificial! Silently drawing your sword, you stand in the shadows and wait. With a whooping cry, a band of dark-skinned warriors clad in panther skins swings down at you from the trees, long knives slashing the air. You are ready for them, though, and leap to the attack. There are five warriors, and they attack two at a time. Each time a warrior falls another takes his place.

PANTHER
  WARRIORS   each   SKILL 5   STAMINA 6

If you take two consecutive hits or your STAMINA score is reduced to 4 or less, turn to **381**. If you defeat the warriors, turn to **155**.

65

With a screaming bellow, a huge Stegosaurus lumbers through the ranks towards you, the Lizard Man on its back howling a blood-curdling war-cry.

STEGOSAURUS　　SKILL 10　　STAMINA 10

Roll one die every round. If you roll 6, you are hit by a sling-stone flung by the Lizard Man rider. Deduct 1 STAMINA point. If you score two consecutive hits against the Stegosaurus, or defeat or kill it, you can flee from it. Roll one die. If you roll 1–2, turn to **187**; 3–4, turn to **144**; 5–6, turn to **47**.

66

'Oho!' comes a deep rumbling voice. You feel yourself hoisted aloft by the collar and slowly turned round until you are staring into the decidedly ugly features of a large Orc. 'A yooman! A yooman!' he yells. The funeral collapses in uproar.

The Shaman yells, 'A sacrifice! A gift to Lord Hashak! Yeah!' Will you try to fight (turn to **265**) or surrender peacefully (turn to **343**)?

67

The narrow tunnel seems to have been formed when part of the roof collapsed into a passage. Before you venture in you poke it with your sword to check that it is safe; it seems so, though a few particles of dust are dislodged. You wriggle in; it doesn't lead very far. At the other end it opens out into a room. You wriggle a little further, the floor beneath you crumbles, and you fall into the room. Turn to **19**.

68

This small alcove was obviously used to store water, wine or something similar, for there are several smashed pots in it. They are of an interestingly ancient design, but don't appear to hold anything of interest. You poke around for a bit but nothing comes to light. Now you may investigate the other alcove (by going to **168**), or leave the room (turn to **274**).

69

The Commander and one of the Swamp Goblins leap to the attack, while the others hastily attempt to put out the flaming pitch and join the battle. They will engage you only if you defeat the first two.

	SKILL	STAMINA
COMMANDER	7	9
First SWAMP GOBLIN	6	5
Second SWAMP GOBLIN	6	5
Third SWAMP GOBLIN	5	5

If you defeat them, turn to **193**.

70

Wiping the sweat from your clammy hands, you grip the pommel of your sword and prepare for battle. You may fight the nightmarish creatures in twos. However, if you should score a hit, their revolting bony frames are so strong that your sword will only cause them to lose 1 STAMINA point.

	SKILL	STAMINA
First ISHKARIM	9	8
Second ISHKARIM	8	9
Third ISHKARIM	7	8
Fourth ISHKARIM	8	10

If you defeat them all, you may take the jewel and leave by the small door to the stairs (turn to **87**).

71

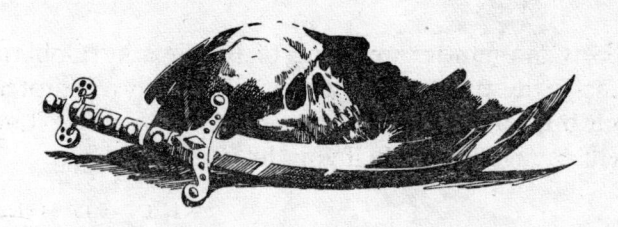

You hear a tremendous thumping sound from the trench, and try to stay as low as you can. A huge riding lizard, along with its Lizard Man rider, leaps the trench and travels on. After dusting yourself down you creep on (turn to **104**).

72

The hours go by. The days go by. No help comes. Soon the vultures will be picking meat from your bones. Your adventure is over.

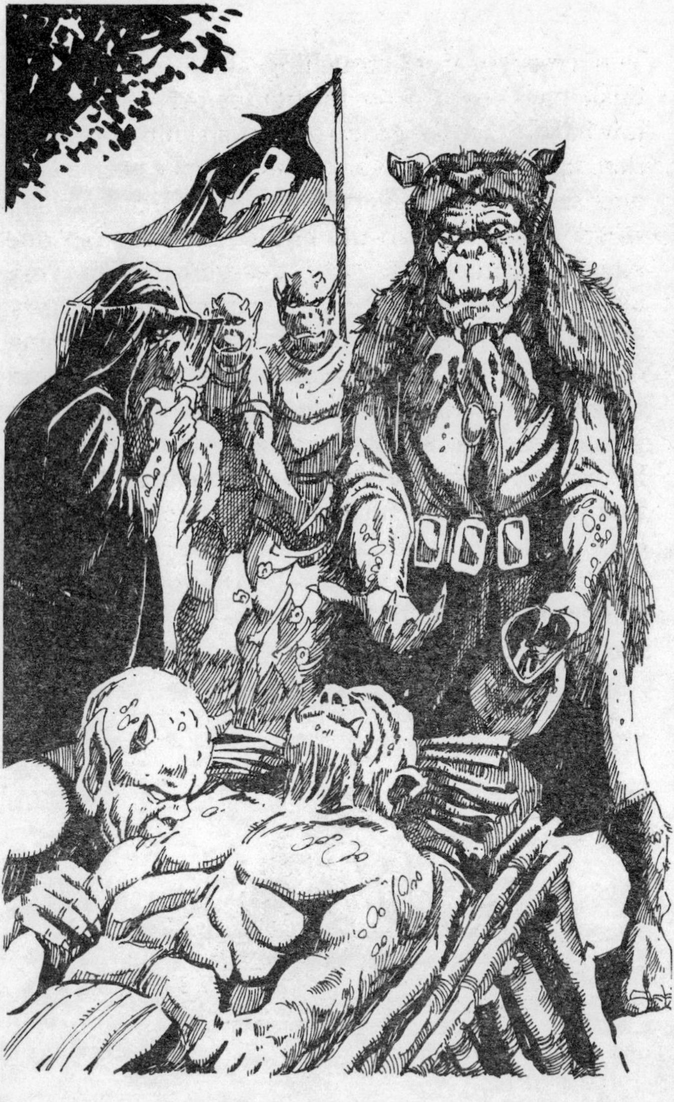

73

You creep nearer, crouching close to some low bushes a little way from the figures. At the top of the low hill you see the group of Orcs all lining up to pay their last respects to what seems to have been a very eminent (but now very dead) old Orc. You slip surreptitiously on to the end of the line. No one pays you much attention; everyone seems very upset and solemn. The dear departed was obviously well loved by these Orcs, as many are weeping openly. The line shuffles on and you get closer and closer to the funeral bier. It is at this moment that you remember sitting with your tutor back in Vymorna, sharing a laugh over the fact that Orc tradition declares that mourners must leave their teeth-marks in the body of the dead! How are you going to get out of this one? Will you attack the nearest Orc (turn to **265**), pretend to bite (turn to **250**), or actually bite the corpse (turn to **392**)?

74

What a magnificent place! Columns stretch out on both sides, disappearing into the shadows, but ahead of you – well, what a sight! The walls are lined with weapons and shields, and carved with murals depicting many great deeds. At their centre, though, stands a magnificent altar to Telak, and upon it stands a small plinth holding a magnificent ruby! Could this be the Eye of Telak? You glance warily around you, peering into the shadows. To one side of the altar there is a small door, obviously leading to the stairs up to the temple where you are to meet Laskar. Will you approach the altar (turn to **229**) or leave by the small door (turn to **87**)?

75

Your equipment and weapons are tossed out to the warriors, and then you are trussed up and carried off to a distant platform high in the trees. There you lie until sunset, immobile and desperately thirsty. As the moon rises you try to relax and sleep but you are very afraid. From beneath you comes the padding of many feet through the undergrowth. You roll to the edge of the platform and peer over. There are a myriad shapes moving about in the moonlight – panthers, dozens of them. Footsteps sound on the platform behind you, something gives you a small push and you fall. The panthers look at you, delicious hunger in their eyes. Claws lash out. Your quest is over.

76

Congratulating yourself, you stride on across the rocky landscape. By the time the sun is starting to set you have descended again to a flat, dusty plain dotted with occasional trees, with the ever-present tangle of jungle away to your right. By now you should really be looking for somewhere safe to spend the night, but nowhere presents itself. And then . . . surely not? A light up ahead, between the trees. You creep closer. Of all the things to find in this forsaken wilderness: a caravan, a gypsy caravan! It stands in the shade of a clump of scrubby trees, an old horse sleepily grazing the rough grass near by. Will you approach the caravan (turn to **268**) or would you rather wait and watch (turn to **366**)?

77

You duck back into the anteroom and cower in the shadows to plan your next move. Suddenly you hear footsteps on the stairs from Telak's temple. The door is flung open and a party of Lizard Men emerge. You have no chance against them – you struggle as they grab you and drag you into the temple before Laskar, but it's no use. The old man turns with a grin of pure malice on his face. One of the Lizard Men hands Laskar a bundle wrapped in cloth. He greedily unwraps it to reveal a gorgeous longsword, obviously the Arm of Telak. 'Now, fool! Do you have the Eyes?' demands the old man in a crazed voice. You reach into your pack and retrieve whatever gemstones you found on your travels. (If you have no gems, turn to 57.) With a disdainful gesture you scatter them across the floor. Laskar dives for them with a mad shout and you lash out at him. Roll two dice. If you roll your SKILL score or less, turn to 46. If you roll more than your SKILL score, turn to 57.

78

A brass-bound door opens to reveal a small passage, which in turn leads to a large room. The chamber is empty of life, but features a row of large stone slabs that look (from the deep red patches splattered on them) as if they were used for dissecting bodies or some similarly gruesome activity. Around the walls lie the shards of smashed pots and vases, but most seem to be filled with ashes – of what, you dare not contemplate! Passages lead off straight ahead and to the right. After peering down both you decide to go right. Turn to 385.

79

'We've got several options,' Lecarte tells you. 'We could make a run for Capra, but the Lizard Men might catch us, especially since we have only one horse. Alternatively, we could wait for them to return and fight them off. Or we could try something else; I have a fire-making substance that I acquired from an old trader of Kallamehr. If we could lure the Lizard Men into a trap and set it off we could wipe 'em off the face of Titan! Now, I'm not sure whether that plan would work at all, so the decision is up to you.' Will you run for it (turn to **120**), stay and fight (turn to **51**) or set a trap (turn to **349**)?

80

You march on, now keeping your eyes peeled for any threat. After an hour passes without incident, you stop and eat some Provisions (if you have any). Your supplies may be getting low. If you want to hunt out some more Provisions, turn to **54**; if you would rather trek on, turn to **257**.

81

Being careful not to trip over the loose rocks, you lead the raging Tyrannosaurus Rex back to the edge of the ridge. If you can get him there before he attacks you, he should distract the Triceratops! As you reach the edge he makes one final lunge for you. *Test your Luck*. If you are Lucky, turn to **34**. If you are Unlucky, turn to **132**.

82

You kick open the door, step through the dark water and trudge up a sloping passageway, leaving wet squelchy footprints behind you. The passage curves round to the right and then the path forks. You may take the right fork (turn to **244**) or the left (turn to **395**).

83

Keeping your head bowed so that your hood covers your features, you lift the chariot for the mutant Lizard Man to refit the wheel. The impatient priest jumps in without thanking you, and cracks his whip for the mutant to pull along again. As the mutant passes you and catches sight of your face, his eyes widen in alarm. You wink at him as he scurries off, his cruel master's whip cracking across his shoulders. Add 1 LUCK point. You move on. Turn to **319**.

84

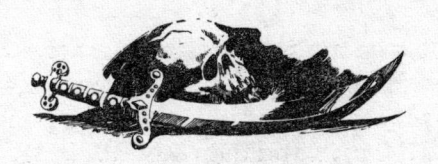

They seem to be waiting too, sitting motionless on their steeds. The peculiar lizards look at you with cold, emotionless eyes. You shudder, as a chill of foreboding grips your body. And then, without a word or movement from their riders, the lizard mounts start slowly to move towards you. Turn to **309**.

85

'Well, at least take something, even if it's only a good-luck charm.' You pore over the big man's wares, which include a pot of black lotus incense; a dazzling square, which Lecarte claims is cloth o' gold; a small idol in the shape of a squat man with a panther's head; a finely worked mace; a jagged copper Orc charm; and a phial of purple liquid. Choose one, then turn to **223**.

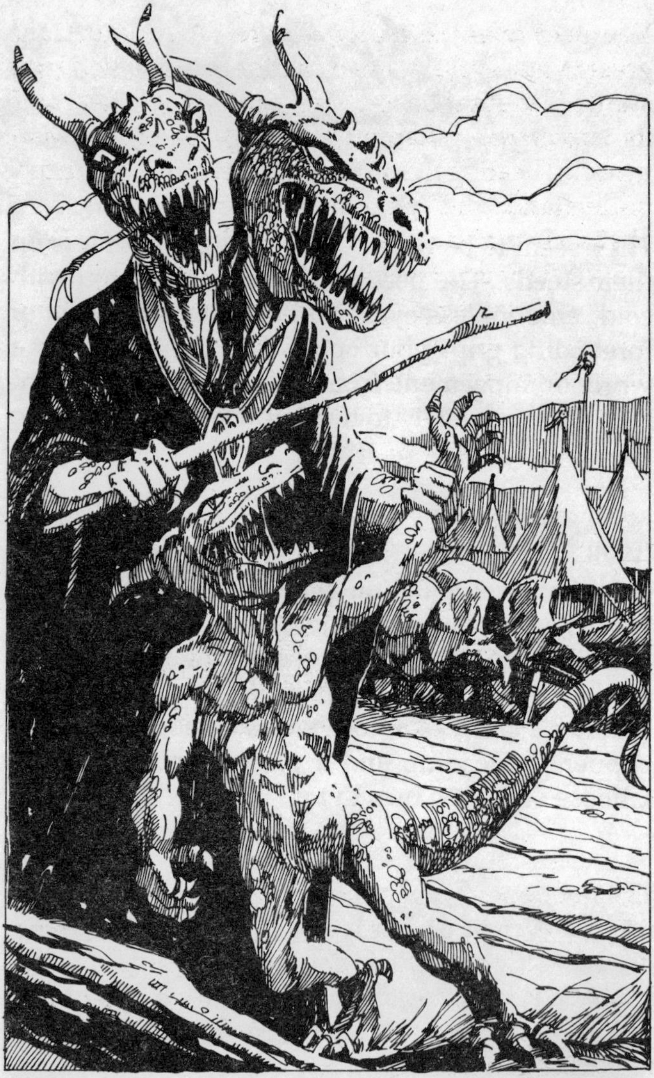

86

You peer over the top of a barrel. A curious sight greets your eyes. A small chariot being pulled by a stunted, mutant Lizard Man has shed a wheel and its passenger, a haughty-looking old Lizard Man priest, is beating the unfortunate creature. You can't understand the words he's saying, but he's obviously furious, alternately shading his eyes from the sunlight and lashing out with a crop. The priest gives an exasperated sigh and gazes around him, obviously looking for someone to assist him. You duck down again, but were you fast enough? *Test your Luck*. If you are Lucky, turn to **134**. If you are Unlucky, turn to **105**.

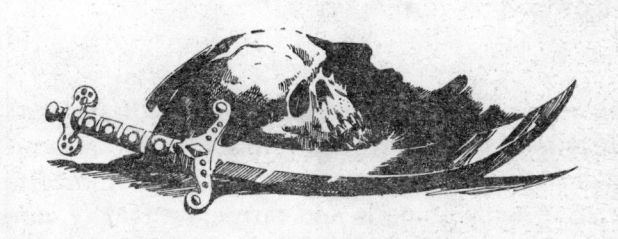

87

The door opens easily enough, leading to a narrow, rough-hewn passageway which slopes up for some distance. Eventually it ends in a small, smooth-walled chamber. Another leads off to your left, but you're more interested in the stairs, which spiral up to Laskar and freedom! Turn to **301**.

88

You grab for your sword and lash out with it, striking at the foul bird as the wind whistles around you!

PTERODACTYL   SKILL 7   STAMINA 9

If you score three hits against the overgrown bird it will drop you – turn to **131**.

89

You reach Capra's welcoming walls and are soon safe behind its thick wooden stockade. It was once a small trading settlement, but now it is crammed to bursting with nomads and farmers afraid of constant attacks by the Lizard Man raiding bands. The townsfolk are stunned by the news of Vymorna, and do all they can to make you feel welcome. All you really want to do is get some rest, but you end up sitting in the Council House for much of the night telling of the siege. Eventually, though, even the anxious relatives clamouring for news of people in the city can see you need some sleep, and leave you alone. Turn to **202**.

90

The door holds. You hear the sound of feet ringing on the stairs behind you. You throw your whole weight against the door again, but to no avail: it won't budge. The other door flies open, and all of a sudden you are being faced by four callously grinning Lizard Men. You must fight them two at a time.

	SKILL	STAMINA
First LIZARD MAN	8	7
Second LIZARD MAN	7	7
Third LIZARD MAN	9	7
Fourth LIZARD MAN	7	8

If you defeat all four opponents, turn to **38**.

91

More by luck than judgement you manage to steer the lizard in the right direction, away from the battle. You leap through the straggling ranks of Lizard Men. In front of you, beyond the last series of barricades and a few amazed soldiers, there is only open country, and freedom. You urge your mount forward, pleading with it to jump the barricades. Roll one die. If you roll 1–5, turn to **263**. If you roll 6, turn to **260**.

92

The sudden light is blinding – but the enormous Black Panther recovers first. Wicked claws slash at you; deduct 2 STAMINA points.

BLACK PANTHER   SKILL 10   STAMINA 10

If you defeat the savage creature, turn to 44.

93

You creep from the castle as the first rays of light are touching the tallest towers. Away to the west you can hear battle being joined as a group of defenders make a suicidal attack on the Lizard Man lines in the hope that they will divert attention away from you. You sneak through the ruined houses down to a conduit, which leads through the lower walls. Soon you'll have to decide whether you are going to head for the plains or the river, but first you must get clear of the city walls! You scuttle through the trenches, hunched in your cloak, until the path divides into two. Will you take the right (turn to 206) or the left path (turn to 296)?

94

Throughout the day Ariella, the sun goddess, blazes down on you. Every step you take is accompanied by a startling screech or growl. You continue to head east, through the ferociously tangled undergrowth. Around noon you have a run-in with a small panther, though the creature scampers away – you don't know who was more terrified, you or it! [**] As the sun starts to sink behind you, you are pleased to hear the sound of the river alongside you, although you can't see it. As you walk on, the ground becomes damp and marshy, and soon you have trouble finding a dry path; you weave this way and that around large, swampy pools and find your feet sinking into the saturated ground. You can try to make camp where you are (turn to **278**), or go on a little way in the hope of finding more solid ground (turn to **378**).

95

You make it, but only just! As you walk down the dark corridor you can still hear the rubble you dislodged bouncing off the wall of the well as it falls into the depths. The passageway ends in five shallow steps, which lead up to another rotting door. From behind it, as you listen, you can hear creaking, like a door blowing in the wind, perhaps. You listen again, but the noise seems to have stopped. You push the door and it gives, but opens with a very loud groan that will guarantee you're not going to surprise the occupants of this room! Turn to **153**.

96

Battered and bruised, blinded by blood pouring from a slash across your forehead, you stagger about in a daze. Someone – or something – batters into you and sends you flying into the midst of the battle. Turn to **144**.

97

You continue on your way, hacking at the tangled undergrowth. The sun rises; the night's animals creep back to their dens to sit out the scorching day in cool shadows. Different creatures screech and chatter in the branches above you. Soon you are bathed in sweat, wishing you could stop, but always pressing on. Turn to **204**.

98

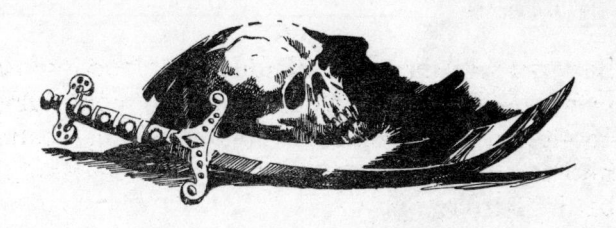

You accompany the strange man as he lays an ambush for the Lizard Men. You can only watch as he picks off two Lizard Men with his arrows. Then, from the low branch of a nearby tree, the Sabre-toothed Tiger leaps down at the inhuman enemy. The mounts of the remaining Lizard Men shy away, turn and run. Snag chases them for a short while, then gives up and returns to the scene of the battle. It sniffs the Lizard Man corpses for a moment before turning up its nose and trotting back to its master. Turn to **240**.

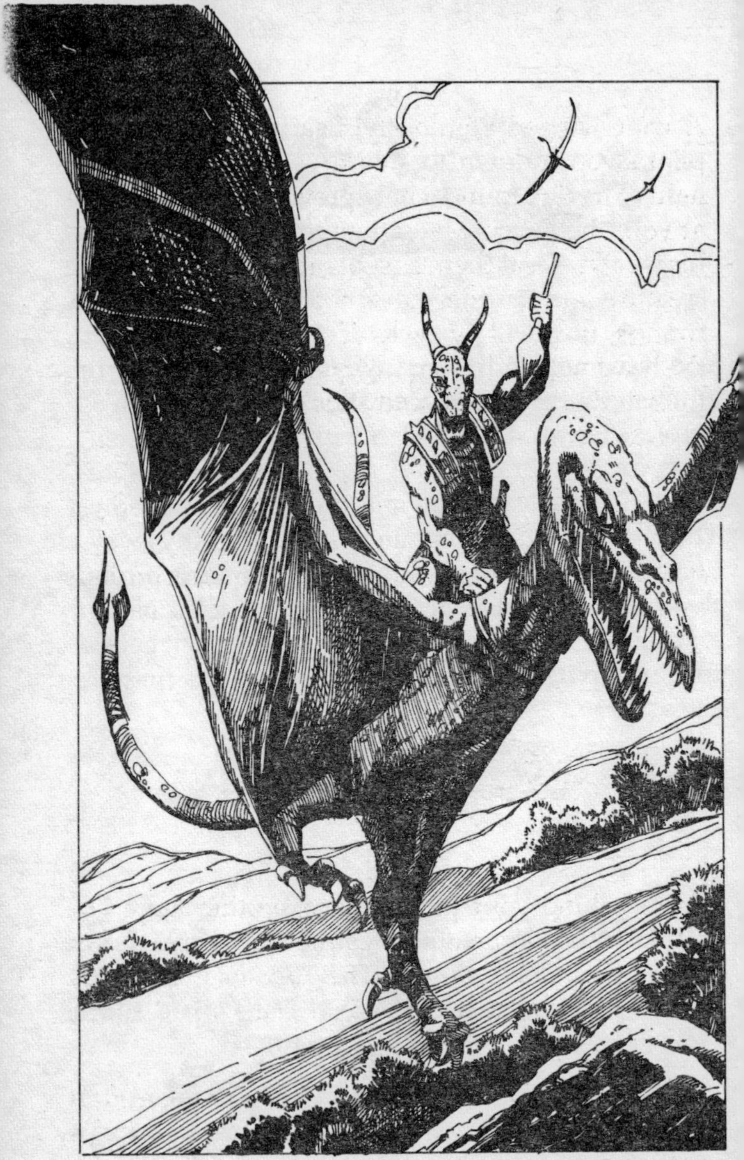

99

A wide-winged Pterodactyl bearing a Lizard Man pilot swoops down to attack, screeching with delight at having found a new prey! Each time it dives at you, the Lizard Man attempts to poke you with his javelin. Treat them as separate opponents. If the creature and its rider have not killed you after six rounds, they will fly away. If you manage to kill it, the beast will flop down to the ground, allowing the Lizard Man to leap off and attack you.

	SKILL	STAMINA
PTERODACTYL	7	9
LIZARD MAN	6	7

If you survive this attack, you may continue on your journey (turn to 164).

100

From behind your hiding-place another large Orc strides up. You breathe a gentle sigh of relief, but keep your head down. The Orc is greeted by another: ''Ello, cuzzin Skaldak. Dat's a bad sniffle yoo got dere.'

'Eh?' replies Skaldak. 'It weren't me oo sneezed. It cum from dat bush dere!' You hear their footsteps getting closer to you. So much for LUCK! Turn to 66.

101

The key fits easily, but requires a lot of forcing to spring the ancient lock. Finally it gives way with a satisfying click, and the box opens to reveal a massive gleaming diamond lying on a base of rotting purple cloth. You gasp in amazement at its size – it must be worth a fortune! Recovering yourself, you secrete the gem in your rucksack, and move on to explore the other room. Turn to 312.

102

You stagger on. The mist is thicker, if anything, than it was before. The ground becomes littered with small white stones and pebbles, which make it increasingly difficult to walk. There's another howl, this time from behind you. Whatever it is, either it circles you – or you are walking round in circles! The rocks crunch beneath your feet and you look down in horror. They are not pebbles: you are walking on bones, a field of small white bones! Shapes loom in the mist around you, accompanied by more heart-chilling howling. Your every instinct is to run, but where to? Will you run (turn to 195) or stay where you are (turn to 39)?

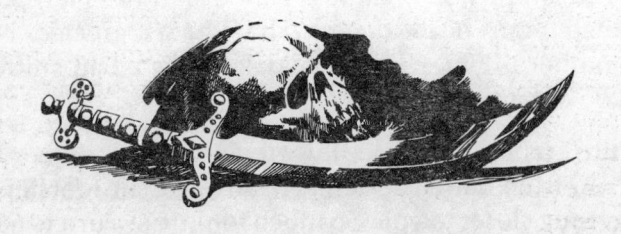

103

You resume your journey, heading due east now. This terrain is very empty, with little sign of life. The land begins to rise. You make camp among a few trees half-way up a rocky hillside, listening to the howls of nocturnal creatures hunting way off in the dark night. In the morning you continue travelling, seeing for the first time the broad band of jungle ahead of you on the horizon. Turn to **377**.

104

This part of the trench has obviously seen some fairly recent fighting, as bloodied bodies lie sprawled in the mud. It seems that a unit of men from the city were holding an important junction against a large force of Orcs and Hobgoblins, but eventually succumbed to superior numbers. There is no sign of anyone around now, though, and you may choose which path to take. You may go left (turn to **18**), right – almost certainly down to the river (turn to **380**) – or take the central trench (turn to **277**).

105

'Grgll'garr! Kffthkr'll!' The old priest has seen you, and is plainly ordering you to help, as his useless servant is now fully occupied in cowering at his scaly feet. You realize that your hood and cloak, together with all the mud plastered over you, must make the short-sighted priest think you are another mutant Lizard Man! There is no time to flee. Will you aid the priest (turn to **283**) or attack him (turn to **157**)?

106

You race down the passage, the fire's heat warming the back of your neck as clouds of smoke billow from the room. The passageway joins a wider tunnel and you run down it, coughing and choking. You run out into a large room and stop to catch your breath – and examine your find. There are several table-like slabs of stone here, obviously used for some grisly purpose, for they all bear the dark brown splatters of ancient blood-stains. You pause by one and carefully unwrap the bundle, shaking it to make sure that no snakes are still hiding in its folds. Inside the bundle, wrapped up in oil-cloth to keep it free from tarnish, is a magnificently decorated sword, engraved and bejewelled, but with something missing from the end of its hilt. What could this be but the Arm of Telak? (Add 2 LUCK points and note it down on your *Adventure Sheet*.) You gaze at the wondrous weapon for a while, before wrapping it up again and strapping it to your back for safety. Now you may leave this chamber by heading left (turn to **385**) or going straight on (turn to **357**).

107

You scull your small craft along the southern side of the river, just out of reach of the branches of the trees overhanging the bank. As you think about them, you realize that you are sailing along the northern edge of the infamous mangrove swamps of Silur Cha, home to the Lizard Man invaders currently pulling down your beloved Vymorna stone by precious stone. The trees begin to look dark and forbidding, holding hidden dangers for you. Will you sail on your present course (turn to **359**) or push out for mid-stream (turn to **12**)?

108

'Why keep silent, young one? You need not fear me, for I serve no one but myself, and mean no harm to anyone because of it. And no one could ever harm me because of it, either. I have made sure of that.' The old man gazes deep into your eyes, and you feel your angry spirit diminishing. You tell White-eye the story of your journey and the siege, and of your hopes and dreams, and more. You talk and talk, feeling somehow compelled to continue. And finally there is nothing more to tell, and you slump in the chair, feeling tricked by this wizened old gypsy. You are not sure what to do; half of you wants to attack him (turn to **285**), while the other half wants to relax and indulge the old man (turn to **391**).

109

The boats draw near. Each holds two grinning Swamp Goblins – they obviously expect an easy victory! You may fight a boatload at a time; each of the three boats holds two Goblins.

	SKILL	STAMINA
First SWAMP GOBLIN	6	5
Second SWAMP GOBLIN	5	5
Third SWAMP GOBLIN	6	5
Fourth SWAMP GOBLIN	5	5
Fifth SWAMP GOBLIN	6	5
Sixth SWAMP GOBLIN	5	5

If you defeat all six Swamp Goblins, turn to **275**.

110

Waving your sword wildly, you attempt to clear a path to the rags. Fight the snakes as one opponent.

TOMB VIPERS   SKILL 7   STAMINA 6

If you defeat them, you manage to get to the pile of rags and clear them of their slithering inhabitants. You grab a large handful of rags, set fire to them and throw them towards the doorway to create a pathway. You grab a second handful, and feel something long and hard wrapped up in the cloth. Hastily tucking it under your arm, you cast more burning rags towards the door, and then make a run for it. You leap the flames, reach the doorway, and fling yourself down the corridor, your heart going fit to burst! Turn to **106**.

111

'Ah, well,' says White-eye, 'so we can't do business. Never mind. Rest now, for it will be light soon enough and you have a long journey still ahead of you.' You take his advice and lie down and close your eyes, but sleep evades you for some time. Just what does the old man know? Eventually, though, you sleep. Turn to **9**.

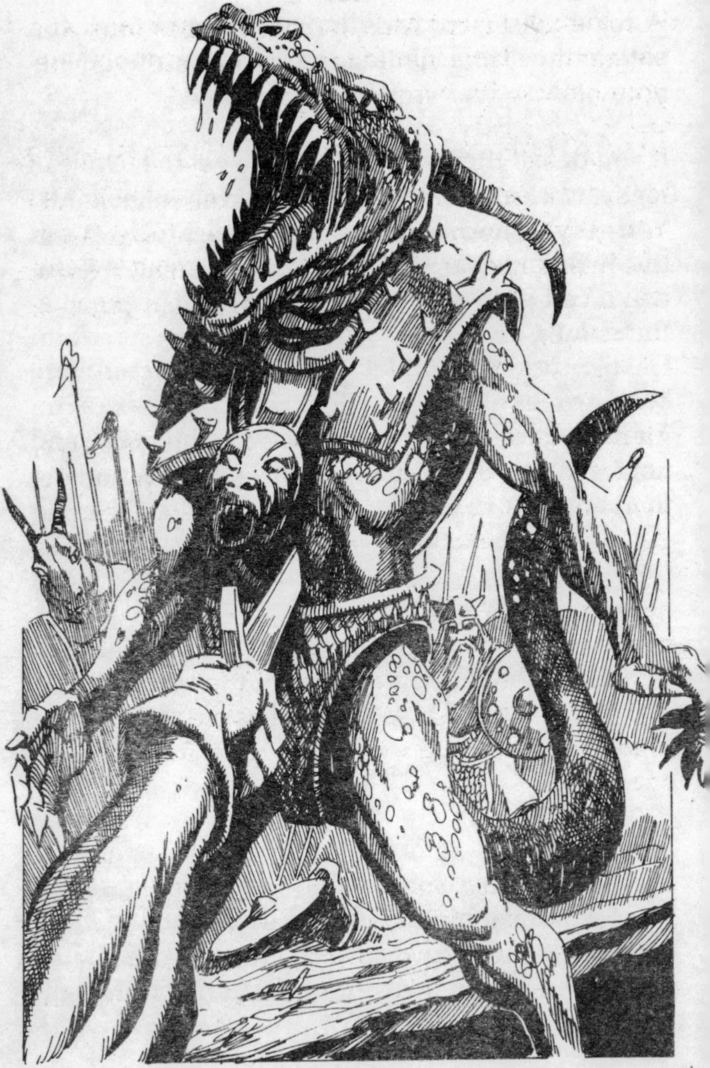

112

A towering Lizard Man warrior crashes into you, swinging a large flint-edged sword and parrying your blows with a crudely made shield.

LIZARD MAN   SKILL 9   STAMINA 10

If the Lizard Man scores two consecutive hits against you, turn to **162**. If you score two consecutive hits against him, or kill your opponent, roll one die. If you roll 1–2, turn to **192**, 3–4, turn to **322**, 5–6, turn to **187**.

113

The messenger, who tells you her name is Katya, agrees to accompany you, but says that her horse is in no shape to be ridden. You set off on foot, leading the ailing beast behind you. That night, you make camp with the dark canopy of the jungle only half a day's walk away on the horizon. The two of you, glad of the company, sit around the fire talking late into the night before sleeping. In the morning you wake to find that Katya's horse has died during the night. You continue your journey on foot. Turn to **272**.

114

You lie stunned in the long grass, temporarily winded by your fall. Looking around you notice a copse only a short way away. Will you attempt to make a run for the trees (turn to **341**), or stand and face the enemy (turn to **189**)?

115

Aiieee! Your hand slips and you slide down the vine, burning several layers of skin off your hand (deduct 1 SKILL point). You land in a heap, disturbing a cloud of flies and butterflies, which buzz around your head before flitting away. You pick yourself up, dust yourself down as best you can and walk on, promising you won't try anything so foolish in the future! Turn to **170**.

116

You creep nearer to the immense siege engine. There seem to be three engineers, Swamp Goblins, commanded by a very officious-looking Lizard Man. They are preparing to fire, lighting huge bales of straw and wood dipped in a cauldron of steaming green pitch. What will you do now? You could sneak away again (turn to **363**), wait for the soldiers to be fully occupied and then leap to the attack (turn to **69**), or if you have your father's bow you could fire one of the special arrows at the pitch (turn to **222**).

117

The ground is very spongy and damp. You sink into it up to your ankles, but luckily no further. After only a few dozen careful paces the ground hardens again and you can go on as before. Turn to **194**.

118

You creep closer, sticking to the bushes. Orcs are lining up to pay their last respects to the body lying on the large funeral bier at the top of the hillock. As you are watching the line shuffle along, a very large Orc comes and stands in silent contemplation right by the bush in which you are hiding! The bush is very prickly, scratching your face and tickling your nose. Suddenly you just know it: you're going to sneeze! Here it comes. Oh, no! Atishoo! *Test your Luck*. If you are Lucky, turn to **100**. If you are Unlucky, turn to **66**.

119

You pull back the remains of the curtain – and come face to face with another Giant Slug! If you are ever going to get out of this room you will have to attack it.

GIANT SLUG   SKILL 7   STAMINA 10

If you defeat it you may enter this alcove (turn to **68**), or leave the room and continue your exploration (turn to **274**).

120

Lecarte looks doubtful, but you set off anyway. The horse is laden with large panniers and bundles of goods, and as a result you make little headway. The shadows lengthen as the sun nears the horizon, but there is still no sign of Capra. Then, from behind you, comes the unmistakable rumbling of hoofs. Looking back, you can count the dark shapes heading straight for you: as well as all the Lizard Men who escaped you earlier, there are another six, quite a force to be taken on by two adventurers and a tiger. Will you continue to run from them (turn to **135**), or turn and fight (turn to **36**)?

121

With a snort the startled Lizard Man wakes up, sees you, and draws a cruelly curving dagger.

LIZARD MAN
  PILOT   SKILL 8   STAMINA 9

If you defeat him, turn to **368**.

122

The ground rises to a small hillock dotted with sparse patches of bushes and trees. At the crest of the hill a motley group stands gathered around a large funeral bier. Looking closely you can see that, despite the veils and dark clothes, the mourners are all Orcs! To one side a bizarrely dressed shaman leaps and capers, throwing bones and entrails to the winds in honour of the dead. In your disguise you could creep closer still and take a better look. While you are deciding, *Test your Luck*. If you are Lucky, turn to **73**. If you are Unlucky, turn to **198**.

123

You come face to face with a dead end as the trench stops in a blank wall. This part must be still under construction. Overhead a huge Pterodactyl wheels above the battlefield, shrieking a ghostly cry. You scurry back to the junction and this time take the left branch. Turn to **18**.

124

You creep round, flat against the wall for the most part, avoiding the rubble and broken fittings. Luckily the Slug seems to be intent on eating the remains of a large tapestry. You reach the rotten curtain covering the first alcove. Will you dart inside (turn to **211**) or attack the repellent creature (turn to **375**)?

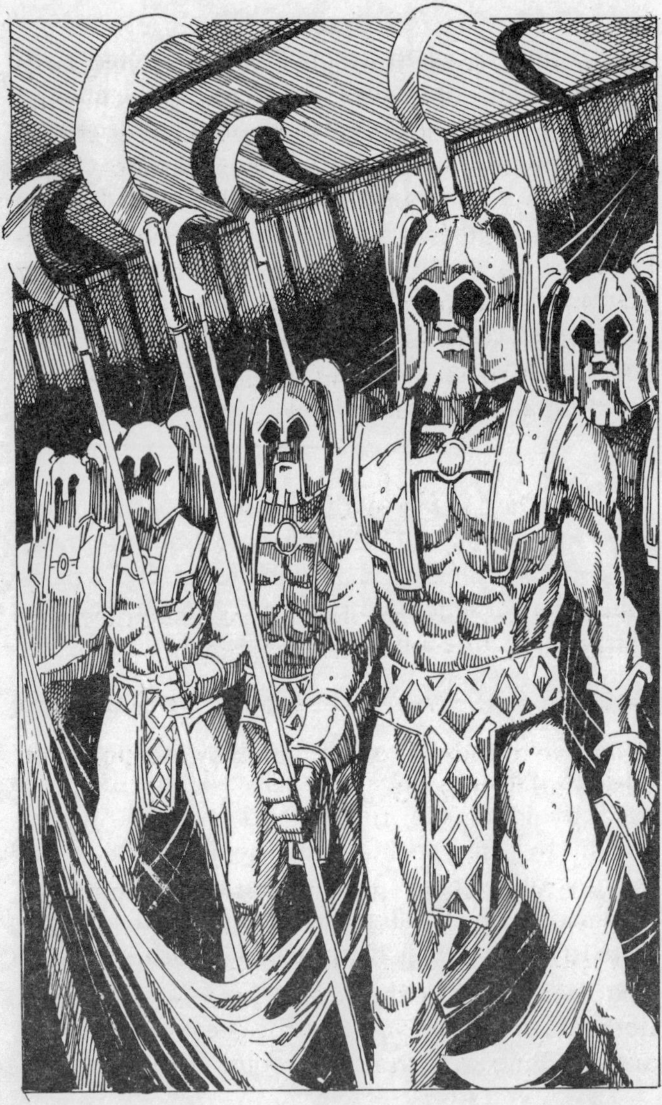

125

The archway leads through to another, very large chamber. You raise your lantern and peer in – and stop in amazement. As far as the eye can see stretch row upon row of petrified stone warriors. Their armour and weapons are detailed and lifelike, though very ancient and foreign in design. So lifelike are they, in fact, that you could almost swear that they were looking back at you! Will you enter and explore (turn to **160**), or retrace your steps and take either the narrow tunnel (turn to **67**) or the right-hand archway (turn to **41**)?

126

You have no chance of fleeing from such teeming numbers! Fight them as one opponent.

WHARF RAT PACK   SKILL 9   STAMINA 11

After five rounds of combat you may escape, if you wish, and turn to **203**.

127

You strike the chest with your sword, try to prise it open with your knife, throw it against the wall, even kick it about a bit but nothing seems even to dent it! You root about in the debris for a key, but find nothing. In disgust you toss the chest into a corner and continue on to the other room. Turn to **312**.

128

You dig for some time, but make no progress. You have moved a fair-sized pile of rocks and debris from the wall, but you seem no nearer to breaking through it. In disgust you give up, collect your things and return to the crypt. You must now choose between going left (turn to **125**) or wriggling down the tunnel (turn to **67**).

129

'What need have I of weapons? I am a man of peace and my friends protect me. Furthermore, I will not trade in weapons of war. I will not trade for this.' White-eye gives you a look that says, 'You should have known better!' Turn to **11** and choose again.

130

It is about half an hour before dawn when you ride out through the shattered main gate of Vymorna with the troop of soldiers who are going to provide an armed escort as far into the enemy lines as they can. The ruins of the outer walls are quiet, save for the feasting of the ever-present vultures and crows. Slowly, picking your way around ruined houses and streets where you used to play, you ride towards the flat, blood-stained plain where the main engagement is to take place. As you leave the ruins behind you peer out across to the sprawling enemy lines. From every side rise soldiers of Evil. They cheer a heart-stopping war-cry, and battle is joined! Turn to **220**.

131

Down, down you fall, the wind whistling through your cape. With an almighty splash you hit the river. For a moment you struggle, before breaking the surface again and gulping in air. You are only a few paces from the shore, and soon you are hauling yourself out. You rest awhile, taking in your surroundings. A little over fifty paces away, a guard stands with his back to you, watching over a host of small boats. If you could steal one you could row up-river with little danger. You might rush the guard (turn to 313), distract him by throwing something like a pebble (turn to 174), or sneak around him through the remains of the old dockside buildings (turn to 158).

132

The Tyrannosaurus Rex is upon you! In vain you try to fend off the cruel snapping jaws, but no matter how hard you fence you cannot win. Soon you will know what few others have known – the inside of a Tyrannosaurus Rex! Your adventure is over.

133

Laskar is still gloating over having you right where he wants you, when a heavily armed band of Lizard Men enter from the back of the temple, presumably having come along the same route as you. Their commander crosses to the old man, carrying a long object wrapped in rags. He speaks with Laskar, who exclaims in your tongue, 'Ha! The Arm of Telak. Now we shall see whether the legends are as true as some believe! You!' – directing his attention to you – 'Give me the gemstones you found on your little, er, excursion!' You have no option but to hand over whatever gems you found on your travels. (If you found none, turn to 57.) You toss the gem or gems on to the floor. Laskar dives for them, a mad gleam in his eye. In a last desperate attempt to be free, you lash out at him with your foot. Roll two dice. If you rolled equal to or less than your SKILL score, turn to 46. If you rolled higher than your SKILL score, turn to 57.

134

Keeping your head down very low, you wait for the noise to die away, before peering out again. The coast is clear and you may move on. Turn to 319.

135

You kick the horse into action but already the Lizard Men are gaining on you. The lights of Capra appear ahead at last, and Lecarte sounds his horn. You are gratified to hear one answer him from the walls of the settlement. Arrows start to whistle around you and you begin to weave about. It will take you twenty rounds to reach the safety of Capra. For each round roll one die. If you roll 6, you are hit by an arrow and must deduct 2 STAMINA points. If you get to Capra alive, turn to **89**.

136

The galley scrapes by, its huge wake soaking you and threatening to capsize your puny craft. As it sails off into the distance – to deliver more supplies and troops for the siege, no doubt – you begin bailing out the water. All your Provisions are ruined (cross them off your *Adventure Sheet*), but otherwise things are all shipshape, and you can sail on. Turn to **376**.

137

You slip round, flat against the wall to avoid being seen by the repulsive creature. In the corner of the room you come across a small metal-bound door. You may go through the door (turn to **355**), or continue round the edge of the room (turn to **329**).

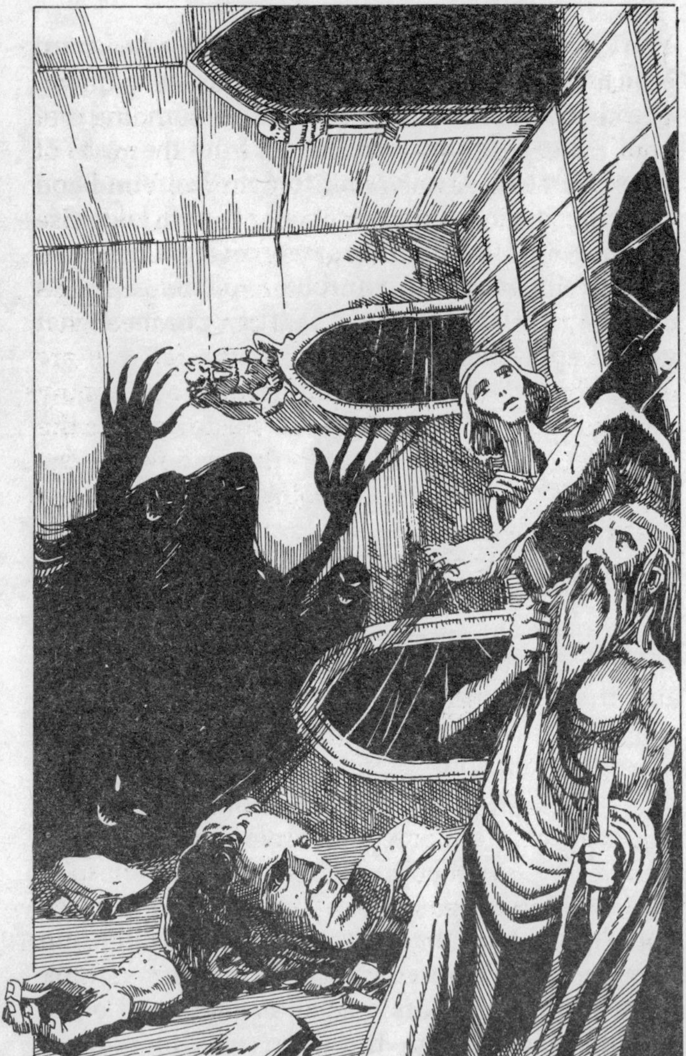

138

You clamber over, around and among the statues, which creak and rock beneath you. Looking down, you see that the one on which you are standing is of your patron, Telak – and that its eyes are made of solid jet. The Eyes of Telak? Of course! You bend down in the flickering light of your lantern and prise out the gems. In the corner of your eye, though, you see the shadows waver and coalesce. Something's watching you! You look up, and can't believe what you can see. Silhouetted against the far wall are evilly shaped shadows, slanting eyes and toothy mouths cut out of them as if the shadows were the creatures. You glance around – the shadows *are* the creatures! You leap up, grabbing your sword. *Test your Luck*. If you are Lucky, turn to **200**. If you are Unlucky, turn to **5**.

139

You leap behind some large rocks as four riders thunder by, swathed in hoods and cloaks despite the heat. You are going to call to them, but then see they are mounted on four-legged riding lizards. No humans would ever be riding such beasts, you think with a smile. The riders head away south, while you continue to head east, more wary of danger now. Turn to **257**.

140

You hesitate a moment, and your eyes widen as you see a large Lizard Man march briskly across to Laskar, talk for a moment, salute and then march back out of your sight. It is a trap! Do you have the Arm of Telak (turn to **373**) or not (turn to **77**)?

141

Lecarte rubs disgusting greeny-brown muddy stuff into your face and hands from a small pot he finds among one of his bundles, and gives you a rough jerkin and leggings to wear under your cloak. 'From a distance,' he assures you, 'you'll pass for a non-human, as long as you don't talk to anyone and don't get too close.' It is now time for you to depart. Turn to **223**.

142

The priest gazes deep into your eyes, and you gaze back. Surely you have seen such eyes before, gazing at you from a Black Panther's face! Could it be that these people are shapechangers, were-men? The priest solemnly picks up your pack and hands it to you, and orders that you be lowered to the ground. Your arms are untied and you are escorted back to where you were first captured. As he turns to go, the priest looks at you, nods, and turns away. Within seconds there is no trace of the Panther Warriors. Add 1 LUCK point and turn to **155**.

143

Do you have anything with which to make a light, something of your father's, perhaps? If you do, turn to **92**. If you do not, you can stay absolutely still (turn to **352**) or you can attack the creature (turn to **225**).

144

Somehow you find yourself cut off from your own side, surrounded by the enemy. All around you mill Trolls, Ogres, Lizard Men, Mutant Orcs and more. For a moment you stagger about in a daze, then a heavy blow smashes across the back of your head. Deduct 2 STAMINA points. If you are still alive, turn to **162**.

145

A horse trots up. Its rider is wearing the uniform of a messenger or scout, and is carrying a bow and a longsword. Both horse and rider seem very tired and dusty from the trail. Will you attack them (turn to **384**), or greet them peacefully (turn to **396**)?

146

The riding lizard is very sure-footed and is soon striding off through open country on its strong hind legs. With your heart still pounding in your chest with excitement, you realize you are free of the city! Add 1 LUCK point, and turn to **53**.

147

Two huge claws grasp your shoulders and wrench you from the ground, high up into the sky. For a moment your mind revolves in sheer panic, but you soon calm yourself, and work out what to do. Will you attack the creature with your sword (turn to **88**) or wait and see what happens to you (turn to **270**)?

148

You creep round the animal pens, noticing with delight that apparently they are not guarded. It should be an easy task to steal one of the riding lizards (turn to **350**). Or would you rather continue on your way out of the Lizard Men's camp (turn to **237**)?

149

The disgusting creature leaps at you, bellowing like a wild boar. She has no weapon, but her fingernails are sharpened into talons. In the confusing fumes of the incense you must reduce your Attack Strength by 1 point for the duration of this fight.

LIZARD WOMAN   SKILL 6   STAMINA 8

If you defeat her, turn to **280**.

150

You hang on to your perch for a while longer, enjoying the breeze. Eventually, though, you must climb down. As you lower yourself through the branches, you notice that there is a clump of long vines hanging from the tree. You are suddenly tempted to swing on one, but would it be safe? Do you want to try (turn to **52**) or would you rather climb down to the ground (turn to **170**)?

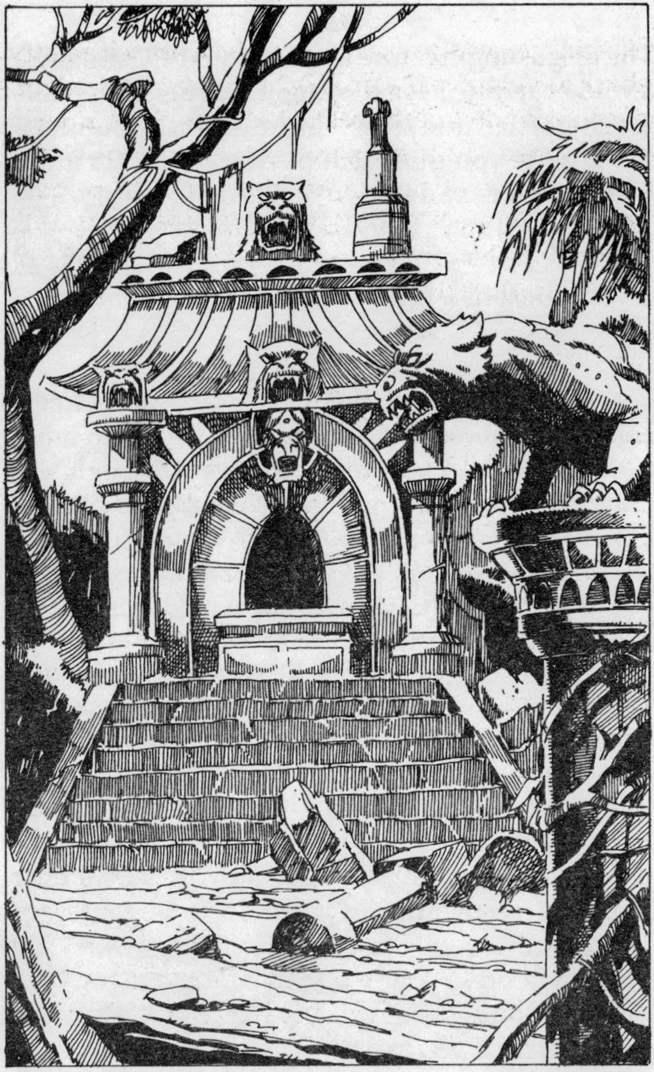

151

Slashing away at the vines, you give yourself a nasty shock as you reveal a large panther-head carved out of some kind of dark rock. These people obviously worshipped a huge panther-god. Between the snarling jaws of the statue, there is a deep, dark hollow. You peer into it, but can see nothing. Will you take a chance and reach into it (turn to **58**), or leave this place (turn to **245**)?

152

This chamber is smaller and more upright than the last. Its walls are lined with shelves, each piled high with musty, rotting ceremonial robes. It seems to be some sort of a dressing-room – the temple to Telak must be very near here. As you search through them, you find some robes in good enough condition to wear. Decide whether you want to wear the robes, and then leave the room by the small door opposite, following the narrow winding passage which leads down to another similar door. You pause and press your ear to the door, but you hear nothing. With your sword at the ready, you push open the door. Turn to **74**.

153

The door opens to reveal a vast hall, its far end shadowy in your flickering lantern-light. You can just make out a large pair of double doors set in the far wall, and a pair of tattered curtains covering two small alcoves on the right wall. More importantly, though, you can also make out the huge grey slug-like creature, which is chomping at one of the curtains! What will you do:

Attack the creature	Turn to 375
Slip round the room's left wall	Turn to 124
Slip round the room's right wall	Turn to 137

154

You pick your way up the stairs, which lie at a terrible, twisted angle, causing you several anxious moments as you drag yourself along. By the top you are walking half on the floor and half on the wall! A small door is set in the wall at the top of the steps, its frame shattered and smashed. You listen at the door but hear nothing except your own heartbeat. Will you enter the room (turn to 311), or would you rather return down the stairs and take the other passage (turn to 353)?

155

You trek onwards, expecting to feel the sting of blow-pipe darts with every step, as the ground rises into the foothills of the Lion Heights. By mid-afternoon the ground is rising steadily and the climb is getting steeper. You stop to eat some Provisions in the shade of a large thorn-bush. As you are sitting munching a large, sweet fruit, you hear a heavy flapping of wings. *Test your Luck*. If you are Lucky, turn to **186**. If you are Unlucky, turn to **99**.

156

In your delusions, you dream of water bathing your face, of standing beneath an ice-cool waterfall . . . You wake in a darkened room, the wizened face of a man staring down at you. You start and try to sit up, but he quietens you, replacing the damp cloth on your forehead. You sleep again. When you wake again, it is still dark, and the old man is still sitting beside you. 'Ah, my young friend,' he purrs. 'Awake at last. Good. I think you should be able to get up now.' He waves a hand towards a pile of your clothes and equipment. 'I found your things scattered in the sand, near where, ummm . . .' His voice trails off in sadness. You try to sit up, and find, to your surprise, that you can. You look at yourself: you are very thin and your skin is peeled and burnt, but otherwise you seem to have made a good recovery (you may replace all but 2 of your lost STAMINA points). Looking around, you discover that you are inside a cluttered caravan. Turn to **61**.

157

Your luck has run out, it seems. The priest peers closely at you, despite the savage sun making him squint. He sees immediately that you are a human, shrieks a curse, and leaps to the attack with his crop!

LIZARD MAN
   PRIEST   SKILL 10   STAMINA 11

If you defeat the priest, turn to **319**.

158

You sneak along through the rubble, nearer and nearer to the boats. *Test your Luck*. If you are Lucky, turn to **181**. If you are Unlucky, turn to **313**.

159

You dive through the door. There is no floor! Roll two dice. If you roll less than or equal to your SKILL score, turn to **386**. If you roll higher than your SKILL score, turn to **55**.

160

You tiptoe through the room of stone warriors, hardly daring to breathe. You feel a thousand pairs of dead eyes on you, but every time you wheel and stare at the figures you see nothing but stone. What you could do with such a force of soldiers! you muse. You leave through the archway at the far end of the chamber, following a wide, dusty passage which leads down and away to the right. Eventually the corridor ends in a largish room. At its centre stand three large stone slabs that appear to have been used for some gruesome practice, for they all bear the dark brown splatters of ancient bloodstains. Beyond speculating as to what went on here there is nothing of interest, and you press on. Will you take the left exit (turn to **385**) or the right (turn to **357**)?

161

You feel very, very ill. The Orcs are all laughing and singing, and showing no ill effects from the repellent stuff, but you feel absolutely dreadful. You wander off and lie down for a bit, your head reeling . . . You wake in a heap on a grassy hillside. Your mouth feels as though a rat has nested in it and you can't focus your eyes! You stand up somehow, and stagger wildly off down the hill to bathe your face in a stream. You feel very groggy, and have a splitting headache. You must temporarily reduce your SKILL score by 2 points. You will recover when you meet this symbol [**] in the text, but not before. You arrange your equipment as best you can and stagger on, now heading east; your path is wooded, with trees all around. At the far end of the woods you pause for breath, but then hear the unmistakable sound of horse's hoofs, getting closer. Turn to **185**.

162

You wake up face down in blood-stained mud, lying sprawled with a number of decaying corpses in the bottom of a trench. Your chest hurts from a deep gash, and there is blood in your hair and a huge bump on your head, but otherwise you seem to be all right. Turn to **333**.

163

'Oh, yeh! Kuzbag's kid! My, 'aven't yoo grown, eh? 'Ow's yer dad?' Before you can answer, luckily, the shaman bellows for everyone to raise a toast to their dear departed chieftain. It strikes you that everyone here has already drunk several dozen toasts, but mugs are passed round, and one is thrust into your hand. You peer in and recoil. It's Guursh, the dreaded Orc ale! Will you refuse to drink (turn to **66**), pretend to drink (turn to **210**), or drink it all (turn to **45**)?

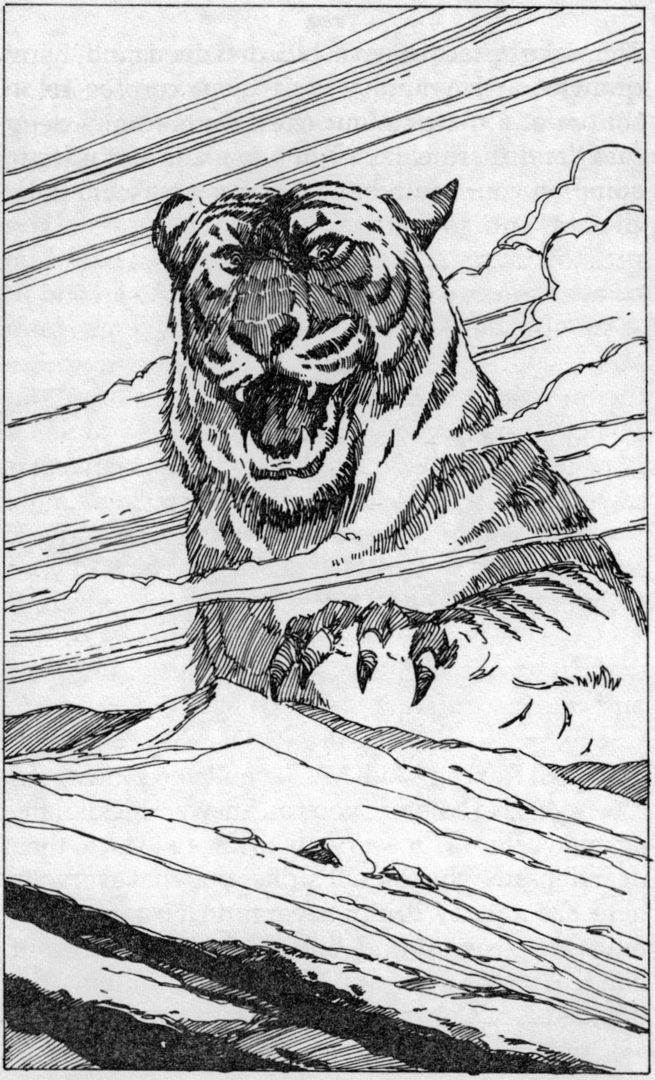

164

There must be a force of Lizard Men near by, you decide – but surely they can't know that you are in the area? You hurry onwards, climbing higher up into the hills. The day begins to wane and you are still climbing. The trees are getting sparser, and the climb is getting harder. Evening comes but you press on, certain that you are close to your goal. You come to a rocky escarpment and start to ascend it. All at once a tremendous howling roar comes from above you. You look up in panic, and see an immense golden tiger dancing in the air above you. Something in the back of your mind tells you that it is an illusion, but your imagination tells you that it is real, and very, very terrifying! Do you remember the stories of the panther-gods of the jungle tribes? Roll two dice; if you roll less than or equal to your SKILL score, you defeat your fear (turn to **239**). If you roll more than your SKILL score, deduct 1 STAMINA point and test again, and again, until you succeed or are literally scared to death!

165

The narrow, rough-hewn passage slopes down for some considerable distance and ends at a narrow doorway. You listen but hear nothing. Carefully, sword at the ready, you push open the door and peer into the room. What a magnificent place! Columns stretch out on both sides, disappearing into the shadows, but ahead of you . . . well, what a sight! The walls are lined with weapons and shields, and carved with murals depicting many great deeds. At their centre, though, stands a magnificent altar to Telak, and upon it stands a small plinth holding a magnificent ruby! Could this be the Eye of Telak? Will you approach the altar (turn to 229) or return to the stairs (turn to 253)?

166

Staggered and shocked by your victory, the ranks of Lizard Men fall back in disarray. Turn to 213.

167

Suddenly you are surrounded by Lizard Men! So much for your brilliant plan! You drop the taper and draw your sword. The reptilian warriors grin and close in on you. Suddenly they shrink back as a horn sounds from the trees, answered by an animal howl. With a yell Lecarte and Snag leap into the clearing. 'Would I let you handle this on your own? And miss all the fun?' Lecarte grins. Turn to 36.

168

This alcove is disappointing, holding nothing but piles of wooden trash – broken and rotten chairs, maybe. You turn to leave and something catches your eye, a glint of lantern-light on metal. Peering back into the room you notice a small crack in the wall. Is there something in there? You squint into the crack: yes, definitely. Something metallic. Will you reach in and grab it (turn to **188**), investigate the other alcove, if you have not done so already (turn to **68**), or leave the room and continue your exploration (turn to **274**)?

169

The sun is setting, and suddenly the jungle is a very cold and unfriendly place. You must find somewhere to sleep before it becomes too dark to see. You could climb up into the branches of a low tree (turn to **218**), or settle down in some soft bushes in the undergrowth (turn to **17**).

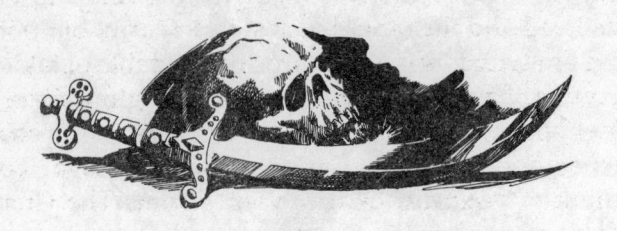

170

The day warms as you journey onward and the jungle comes alive. Birds call, monkeys scamper in the trees, everywhere is strangely beautiful. A new call, one you have never heard before, sounds way up ahead, and is answered by a roar: some overzealous parrot eaten by a crafty jaguar, no doubt. But on the other hand . . . Roll two dice. If you roll less than or equal to your SKILL score, turn to **64**. If you roll higher than your SKILL score, turn to **320**.

171

The path curves gently down between rows of ancient statues before opening out into a large antechamber littered with debris. Opposite are a pair of solid double doors. You cross to them and listen carefully, but hear nothing. Gingerly, you push them open and peer into the darkness. The next chamber is similar to the last, but larger and in better condition. In each corner stands the life-sized statue of a warrior, with two more flanking the doors at the far end of the room. You pick your way across the room, and almost jump out of your skin in fright as the two door Guardians cross spears to bar your way! The one to the right is missing most of its head and the other has lost its left arm, but both are animated by Evil and are quite capable of taking you on. The head on the floor by the right warrior's feet booms out: 'None shall enter here! None shall enter here!' It's just like an old heroic saga, you think to yourself, hefting your sword. The Guardians attack together.

	SKILL	STAMINA
First GUARDIAN	6	4
Second GUARDIAN	5	5

If you defeat both of them, turn to **269**.

172

A grotesque, subhuman Ogre shambles across towards you, swinging an immense jawbone as a club.

OGRE	SKILL 7	STAMINA 10

If it scores two consecutive hits against you, turn to **306**. If you score two consecutive hits, or kill the Ogre, roll one die. If you roll 1–2, turn to **65**; 3–4, turn to **208**; 5–6, turn to **382**.

173

The two coal-black gems fit into the hilt of the sword where they rattle loosely. You leap for Laskar, swinging wildly with Telak's sword. He looks terrified, but somehow parries your blow with his staff. Where is the immense power this sword is meant to have? you wonder. An arrow thuds into your arm, and another into your leg. You fall to the ground and a Lizard Man's sword swings towards your neck. Your adventure is over.

174

You toss a rock towards the far side of the quay. Roll two dice. If you roll less than or equal to your SKILL score, turn to **181**. If you roll higher than your SKILL score, turn to **313**.

175

You plunge into the green leafy darkness of the jungle. Little light penetrates here, but eventually you grow accustomed to it. Your eyes start picking out hanging vines, birds high up in the lofty trees, monkeys swinging and chattering with one another. It is the cries of the creatures that are most surprising. From up ahead a peculiar roaring echoes through the trees. Will you go on (turn to **330**), or retrace your steps and head north (turn to **27**)?

176

The band consists of four mounted riders, cloaked and hooded despite the scorching heat, riding four-legged lizard mounts. There's no chance for either of you to hide now, even if you wanted to. The mysterious riders slow and trot to a halt at a wary distance from you. You cannot see their faces and there is no indication of who or what they are. Will you greet them (turn to **22**), attack them (turn to **247**), or wait for them to make a move (turn to **24**)?

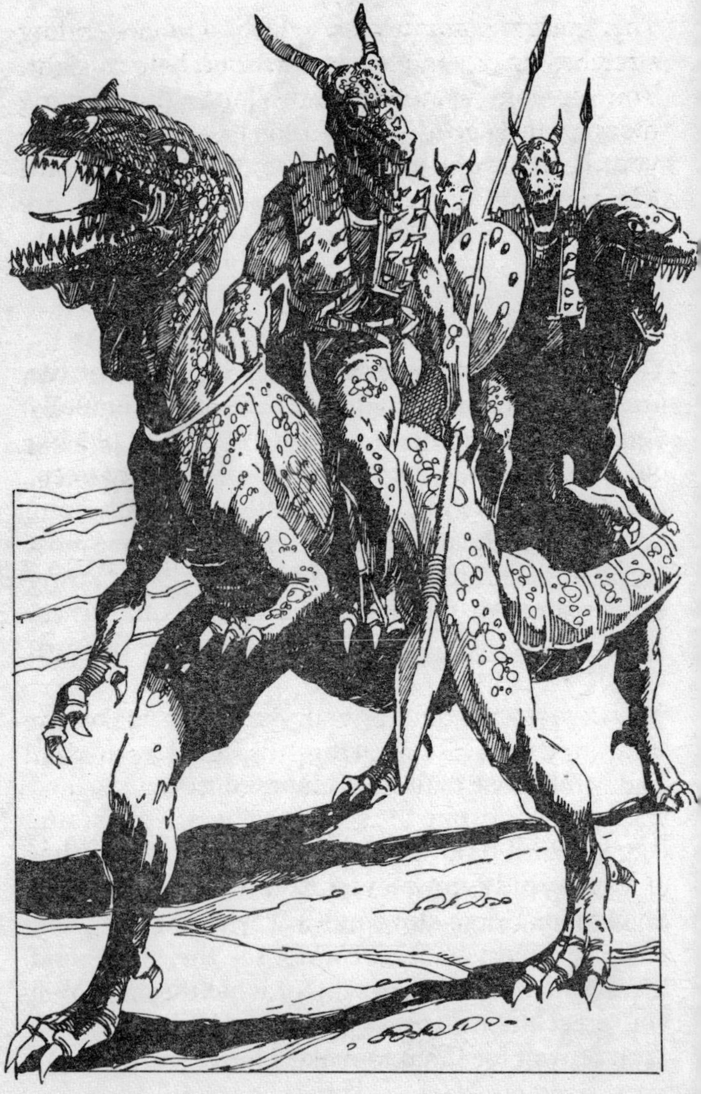

177

The grassy plain across which you are riding stretches on for an eternity, with no help in sight. You race on, wondering how long your panting mount can keep up this furious pace. You crane your head around and look behind you: the Lizard Men are gaining on you! *Test your Luck*. If you are Lucky, turn to **347**. If you are Unlucky, turn to **399**.

178

You creep along, flattened against the wall. As the Orc sneaks round the other side of the building, you let out a sigh of relief and turn to hurry away. Slam! Straight into the chest of the other Orc! He looks down at you with his little piggy eyes and growls. You must fight him.

MARSH ORC   SKILL 6   STAMINA 7

If you defeat him, turn to **32**.

179

You dive for the door but fall short. The snakes are all around you, hissing at the prospect of fresh meat! Fight them as if they were one opponent.

TOMB VIPERS   SKILL 8   STAMINA 11

If you win, you beat a way to the door and escape from this room of nightmares. Turn to **29**.

180

You swing across the glade and land on what appears to be a wooden platform, woven from branches and perched high up in the trees. A narrow walkway leads off it. Will you follow it (turn to **33**), or swing down to the ground on the rope and continue your journey on foot (turn to **170**)?

181

You reach the boat with ease. Hastily throwing your equipment into a corner, you push the small craft out into the river. You're free of Vymorna! Add 2 LUCK points. The Vymorn River is broad and slow-moving. Its name means 'Dark Waters', for it carries black silt washed down from the Lion Heights far to the east – which is where you are headed. Which course will you follow as you row up-river? Will you hug the north bank (turn to **314**), the south bank (turn to **107**), or travel mid-stream (turn to **12**)?

182

You creep carefully up the steps, which are twisted and buckled. They curve slightly to the right as you climb. When you are nearly at the top you hear a noise from behind you, back in the room, which makes you pause. You listen carefully, and hear strange, guttural voices. Lizard Men! You run up the last few steps, through the door at the top and slam it behind you. To your alarm you notice that there is no lock, and gazing around, you can see nothing to bar it with either. In blind terror you race down the corridor, pausing only to notice that on both sides it is lined with barred cells. There is another door at the far end. You kick it – and it holds firm. It's locked! Your heart sinks. Will you try to force it again (turn to **321**), or look for a key (turn to **264**)?

183

You pull back the remains of the curtain – and come face to face with another Giant Slug! If you are ever going to get out of this room you will have to attack it.

GIANT SLUG   SKILL 7   STAMINA 10

If you defeat it you may enter the other alcove, if you have not done so already (turn to **68**), or leave the room and continue your exploration (turn to **274**).

184

You are buffeted by giant gusts of wind, and then hear the man next to you scream in terror as he is dragged aloft by a Pterodactyl. You stare after the unfortunate man for a moment, and then return your attention to the battle just as an immense blood-spattered Troll barges his way towards you.

TROLL WARRIOR   SKILL 9   STAMINA 9

If your opponent scores two consecutive hits against you, turn to **162**. If you score two consecutive hits against him or kill him, turn to **333**.

185

The sound of hoofs comes closer and closer, but they slow to a gentle trot as they approach the trees. Will you leap out and challenge the rider (turn to **302**), or wait and see what happens (turn to **145**)?

186

You leap into the cover of the trees as a huge Pterodactyl bearing a Lizard Man pilot swoops low overhead. If you have your father's bow and arrows you may attempt a shot (turn to **318**). Otherwise you can only watch the beast fly off into the distance, before moving on (turn to **164**).

187

Two gibbering Swamp Goblins, both dressed in the livery of the Lizard King's army, leap for you brandishing tiny jagged knives. You must fight both at once.

	SKILL	STAMINA
First SWAMP GOBLIN	5	5
Second SWAMP GOBLIN	6	5

If they score two consecutive hits against you (either singly or between them), turn to **162**. If you score two consecutive hits against either of them, or kill both outright, roll one die. If you roll 1–2, turn to **208**; 3–4, turn to **172**; 5–6, turn to **65**.

188

Gritting your teeth to steady your jangling nerves, you reach into the crack. *Test your Luck*. If you are Lucky, turn to **215**. If you are Unlucky, turn to **346**.

189

The Lizard Men ride up – all eight of them! They grin arrogantly at you as you stand, sword drawn to face them. They kick their mounts and advance towards you, curved blades at the ready. There is no escape. Your adventure is at an end.

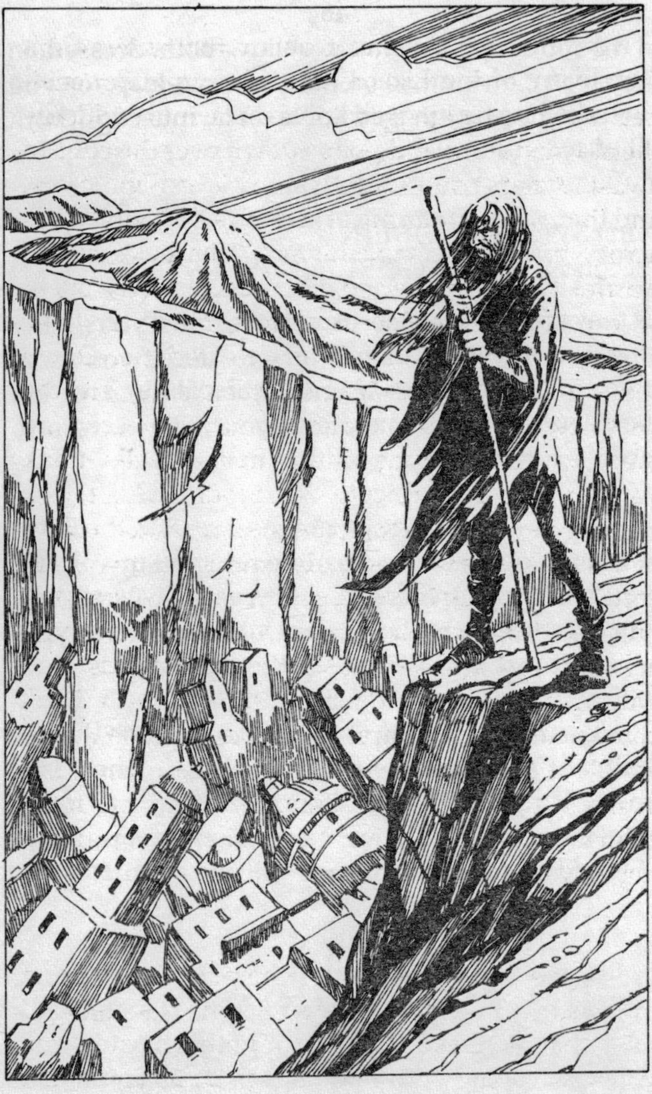

190

In the morning Laskar asks you to follow him from the cavern, making no mention of last night's activities. You climb high up into the hills until suddenly the old man stops and points down over the edge of a vast ravine. You look to where his arm indicates, and find yourself staring at an entire city, which lies across the floor of the ravine. 'Kharnek, city of warrior-kings, now accursed,' he says. 'I've spent all my life in studying its secrets, but there have always been places that have defeated me. Down there, in the depths of the royal palace, are the deathless ones, the warriors who will sleep no more. I am too old for combat, but you, well, I think you will be safe. Down there somewhere, the legends have always said, are the Arm and the Eyes of Telak, the great hope from your dreams. I am certain that the Arm is a huge bejewelled sword, but I do not know what form the Eyes take. When you are ready, we will descend to the upper levels. You will enter there and do what you have to do. I will climb up and meet you at the temple high on the far wall.' He indicates it with a bony finger. 'There is a stair which leads up to it from behind the main chapel to Telak, I believe. Now,' says Laskar, turning to go, 'let us see what you will need.' Turn to **48**.

191

White-eye leans over and whispers, as if being overheard. 'I have heard that Laskar is a changed man, that he gives allegiance to another master from yours. Go along with him only as far as you must, and be prepared for treachery! Now, man-child, sleep.' You lie back, puzzling over what you have heard and dreading what you still have to do. Eventually, sleep comes to you. Turn to **9**.

192

A hail of arrows lands all around you. Men fall, the cruel barbed shafts pinning them to the blood-caked earth. Roll one die. If you roll 1–4, none of the arrows hit you. If you roll 5–6, though, deduct 2 STAMINA points as one wings your shoulder. The press of battle returns and another opponent leaps towards you. Roll one die. If you roll 1–2, turn to **208**; 3–4, turn to **47**; 5–6, turn to **333**.

193

You pour the pitch and bales of straw and wood all over the siege engine, and toss a blazing torch on to it. It burns satisfyingly rapidly. At least that's one catapult that won't be bombarding your beloved Vymorna any more. Add 1 LUCK point. Turn to **363**.

194

Noon passes into afternoon, and you continue to hack your way through the tightly packed vegetation. As the sun starts to cool you can stop and eat some Provisions. If you have none, you may search for more (turn to **374**), unless you would rather continue walking (turn to **169**).

195

You turn and flee but the voices and faces are all around you. You clutch your head and scream but no sound emerges. Dead faces loom out of the mist; swords and axes wielded by skeletal hands scythe the air. You fall to your knees in sheer terror. The roar of battle is all around. Metal clashes on metal and bone; screams and curses howl in your ear. The grinning death's-head faces of warriors long dead close in around your whimpering frame. Soon you will join their legion. Your quest is at an end.

196

The passage leads only a few paces before opening out into another badly damaged room. Religious relics, pots, robes and boxes lie smashed across the floor. As you gaze around, though, your eye lights on a chest sitting in a corner, almost completely unscarred. Do you investigate further (turn to 335), or would you rather leave this room and move to the other (turn to 312)?

197

The emeralds flip out of the crown. Rather strangely, both have flat backs, but when you hold them up together you see why – they are two halves of the same huge stone. Congratulating yourself on the discovery, you secrete them in your rucksack (note them down on your *Adventure Sheet*) and move on. Turn to 310.

198

'Aha!' comes a rumbling voice in your ear. ''Ello, bit shy are yer? Cum to pay yor larst respeks, too? Cum on then, Cuzzin!' A very large and ugly Orc reeking of alcohol slaps you on the back and ushers you forward up to the top of the hill. 'We're all family 'ere, y'know. No standin' on ce-ree-mon-ee or shyness.' Will you go along with this for the moment (turn to **287**), or try to escape by kicking the Orc somewhere you hope he still has some feeling left and run away (turn to **230**)?

199

You creep over the bridge and find yourself on a larger platform, from which lead a great number of covered hollows. You peer into one, and find it laid out like the inside of a hut, with straw bedding and furs placed on the floor. Then you stiffen – a sliver of cold metal has just been placed against your neck! You duck and kick out, sending a warrior flying off the edge of the platform to fall to his doom. However, there are five other warriors and they are ready for you. Roll two dice. If you roll less than or equal to your SKILL score, turn to **292**. If you roll higher than your SKILL score, turn to **324**.

200

You trip and knock over your lantern, but luckily it stays lit. The sinister Shadow Ghouls creep across towards you, flickering in the light. You must fight all three at once!

	SKILL	STAMINA
First SHADOW GHOUL	8	4
Second SHADOW GHOUL	8	5
Third SHADOW GHOUL	7	5

If you defeat the creatures, turn to **337**.

201

You spur your mount on, but it is worn out from the chase and gives way under you. As you fall, your leg gets trapped under its body and you cry out in pain. Deduct 1 STAMINA point. By the time you have extricated yourself from the tangles of the saddle and stirrups it is too late to run. Turn to **189**.

202

Before the first silver fingers of dawn are in the sky you are up and about, preparing to continue your journey. Despite the dewy mist that clings to everything, you must be off quickly. From what the townsfolk have told you, the best route seems to be to head north and then slowly veer due east. Lecarte helps you get ready. While he helps you pack your things (including 2 Provisions the townsfolk found somewhere), he tells you he has another plan. 'Howsabout you adopt a disguise? Make yourself less human-looking, eh?' Will you decide to go on in disguise (turn to **141**), or reject the idea (turn to **85**)?

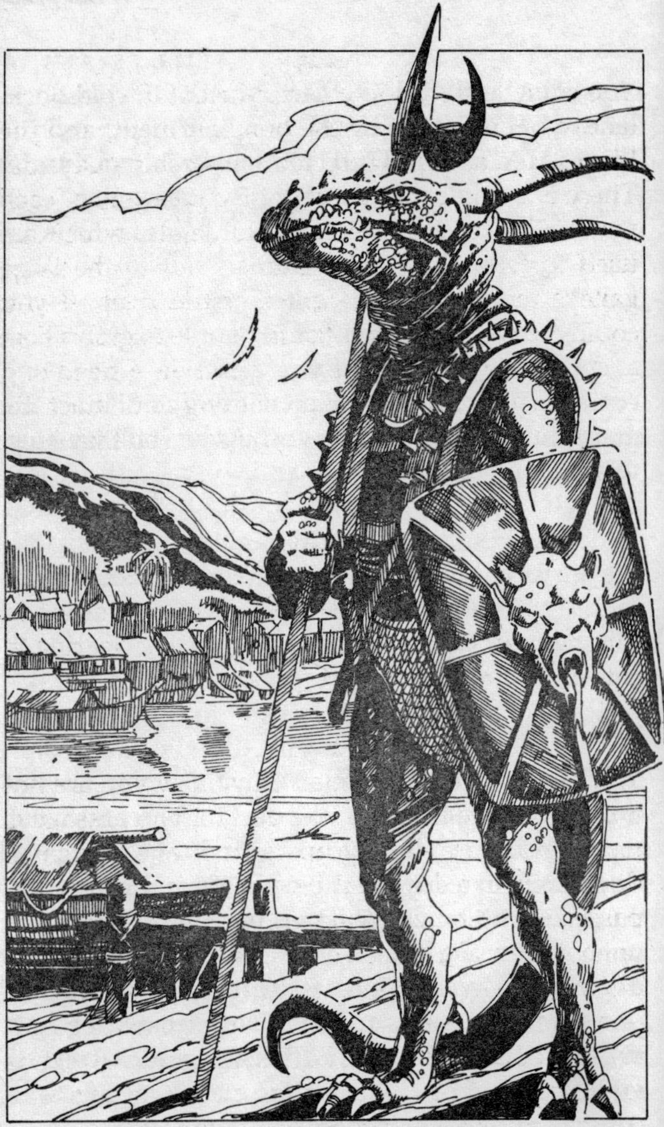

203

You come to the wide wharf. Most of the old dockland was destroyed by the bombardment, and the Lizard Men have now erected a makeshift quayside. There is a single guard every fifty paces or so, each watching over a cluster of small boats, which are used to ferry men and materials out to the large galleys moored in the centre of the river. If you could distract one, you should be able to grab a boat and head up-river. Will you attack in a headlong rush (turn to 313), throw something to distract the guard (turn to 174), or try to sneak up on him (turn to 158)?

204

It's no good – you simply must rest after your rough night. You collect more Provisions and sit down in the shadows at the edge of a small sunlit clearing to eat. Turn to 307.

205

You make it – but only just! Obviously you are not much good at jumping, you decide! The passage is narrow, sloping slightly upwards to end in a small door much like the one through which you recently passed. After much creaking resistance, you pull it open, to reveal a largish chamber lined with murals depicting legendary events. An altar is situated to one side, but seems to have lain unused for centuries, if the build-up of ancient spiders' webs is anything to go by. At the far end is an archway covered by an archaic rotting curtain. Turn to 14.

206

Picking your way over grisly bodies, you sneak off along the trench. The floor of the trench seems to rise, for you are soon having to crouch further and further down to stay below the edge. A screeching, stomping noise makes you halt in your tracks as it gets nearer and nearer. Will you peer over the edge of the trench to see what it is (turn to **231**), or keep your head down (turn to **71**)?

207

You slip carefully down the steep slope, but your feet dislodge small stones, which bounce noisily down ahead of you. The Triceratops stops eating and lumbers towards you with a bellow.

TRICERATOPS   SKILL 12   STAMINA 18

The Triceratops has two attacks; treat the second attack as if you were being attacked by a second opponent with the same SKILL score. If you defeat the creature, turn to **76**.

208

'Ha! Yes indeed, ha!' There before you is a creature much like a stunted Two-headed Lizard Man – a Calacorm! Muttering to itself about what it's going to do to you, it leaps towards you. The Calacorm has two attacks; treat the second attack as if you were being attacked by a second opponent with the same SKILL score.

CALACORM   SKILL 6   STAMINA 8

If it scores two consecutive hits against you, turn to **306**. If you score two consecutive hits against it, or kill it, roll one die. If you roll 1–2, turn to **47**; 3–4, turn to **333**; 5–6, turn to **213**.

209

You reach the trees, shouting appalling curses at the man, who reveals himself to be wild-eyed and tough-looking, dressed in furs and leathers. 'You stupid son of a bristle-beast, you shot my mount! Now what am I going to do?' you scream, quite livid with anger. The man calmly peers out at your pursuers, then turns towards you. Turn to **21**.

210

You lift the earthenware mug to your lips and make the ritual slurping sounds. You think you've got away with it, but your Orc companion, having finished his mug in one go, helpfully lifts the base of your cup for the gruesome liquid to flow into your mouth. You have no option now but to drink! Turn to **45**.

211

You lift the curtain and creep towards the other alcove, but the Giant Slug has seen you and slithers forward, its huge maw drooling saliva and slime. Ready your sword and turn to **375**.

212

Your shot rings true and one of the Swamp Goblins falls lifeless into the water. The other boats draw near, though, and you must fight them, a boatful at a time. This is not going to be an easy battle.

	SKILL	STAMINA
First SWAMP GOBLIN	6	5
Second SWAMP GOBLIN	5	5
Third SWAMP GOBLIN	5	5
Fourth SWAMP GOBLIN	6	5
Fifth SWAMP GOBLIN	5	5

If somehow you defeat all the raiders, turn to **275**.

213

You see a chance, a weakness in the enemy lines. Screaming for everyone to follow you, you make a mad dash straight at the ranks of heavily armed warriors ahead of you. Roll two dice. If you roll less than or equal to your SKILL score, turn to **23**. If you roll higher than your SKILL score, turn to **288**.

214

Shouting wildly to Lecarte to 'Get the heck out of here!', you race for the trees with your taper. Rushing through the darkness you head for the clearing – and the Lizard Men. *Test your Luck*. If you are Lucky, turn to **63**. If you are Unlucky, turn to **167**.

215

Your hand closes on the object and you pull it out. It is a gleaming key that would fit a Z-shaped lock. You slip it into your pocket, praising your good luck and hoping it will come in useful. Now you may explore the other alcove, if you have not done so already (turn to **119**), or leave the room and continue your explorations (turn to **183**).

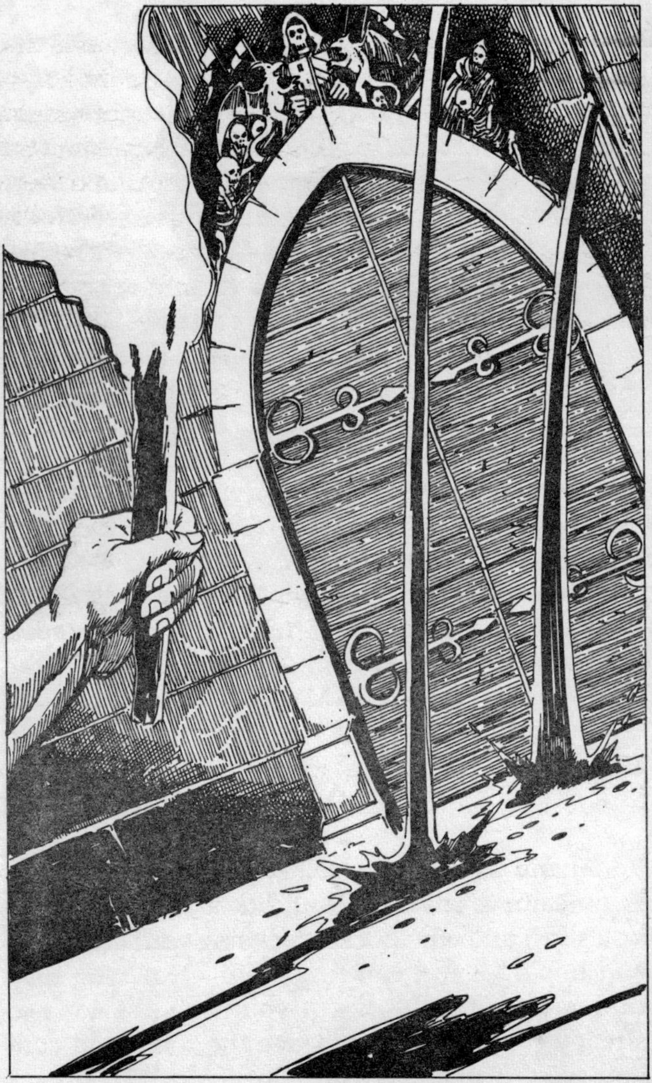

216

The door flies open and you dart through, along another short corridor and to another door. As you reach it you kick it open, leap into the room beyond and slam the door. You pause for a moment to collect yourself, close your eyes and take a deep breath. Then you open them! Your feet are getting wet. You gaze around in panic – the room is leaking! Blood-red water is pouring into the room through cracks in the walls and ceiling. Blood-red water? Oh, Telak! It *is* blood – the room is *bleeding*! What sort of corrupt evil has infested this place to cause this? As your mind reels you are distinctly aware of thumps against the door. It flies open, and four Lizard Men stride in. Momentarily confused by the strange angle of the room, and its disturbing contents, they quickly recover and leap to the attack. You must fight them two at a time; because of the conditions, you must all fight with 2 deducted from your Attack Strength.

	SKILL	STAMINA
First LIZARD MAN	8	10
Second LIZARD MAN	9	9
Third LIZARD MAN	8	8
Fourth LIZARD MAN	9	9

If you defeat the Lizard Men, turn to **82**.

217

Immediately there are dozens of swords and notched arrows pointing at your neck, and each weapon is held by a coolly grinning Lizard Man. It was a trap! Laskar turns, a look of delighted malice on his twisted face. 'Ha! So you are here, you young dupe! Do you have with you the Arm of Telak?' Well, do you have the sword (turn to 248) or not (turn to 133)?

218

You pull yourself up into the spread branches of a tree, brush off a few spiders and bugs, and settle down to sleep, wrapped in your cloak and listening to the chirping of the nocturnal insects. Turn to 56.

219

You awake with a start and try unsuccessfully to sit up. You struggle, but find you cannot move anything except your eyelids, as you are trapped inside a huge, matted spider's web. You curse and wriggle, but to no avail. Then you see the Spider! It is easily the same size as your head, covered in black and orange stripes like those of a wasp. It wriggles down until it is perched on your chest, and stares at you. Will you struggle to pull yourself free (turn to 235), strain to reach the dagger at your belt (turn to 370), or lie still (turn to 291)?

220

Screaming with one voice, the hordes of Evil race across the battle-plain. Carrion-crows and vultures rise into the air above them, screeching in anticipation. The first shock waves ripple through the lines as the sides meet, and for a moment everything is utter confusion. You were warned to stay near the rear of the force, but now you must face an opponent – though in the confusion you won't know who it is until you are confronting them! Turn to one of the following: **10**, **112**, **172**, **187**, **322** or **382**.

221

Reminding yourself to be more vigilant in future, you march on, hacking your way through the jungle's tangled undergrowth. The going becomes easier as you find the rhythm again, but you will never be used to having to slash a path for yourself. Turn to **94**.

222

Varooomm! Your arrow strikes the virulent pitch, which explodes in an immense cloud of flame and decimates the area. You hurry away from the smouldering ruins of the siege engine, congratulating yourself on a job well done. Add 1 LUCK point and turn to **363**.

223

As you depart, Lecarte leans over and embraces you, and whispers in your ear: 'Search out Whiteeye. He'll help you, I'm sure of it. But don't mention I told you so, all right?'

'What about you, Lecarte?' you ask. He tells you he's going to head further west, searching for news of his father. You bid him farewell and set off again. Are you going to head north (turn to **300**) or east (turn to **251**)?

224

You have time to fire one arrow. It flies true and hits its target in the amorphous head region. The creature screams, and lunges for you.

GIANT SLUG   SKILL 6   STAMINA 8

If you defeat the Giant Slug, turn to **362**.

225

Your mind racing, you realize there's no room to swing a sword up here, and carefully unsheathe your knife. You are just about to strike when the moon comes out from behind a cloud, affording you a glimpse of the creature. It's an enormous Panther, black as night, and it is dragging the body of a small deer up into the tree to eat. As you gaze at it, you realize the creature is staring at you! The moonlight glints on your knife, and then on the claws of the Panther.

BLACK PANTHER   SKILL 10   STAMINA 10

If you win the battle, turn to 44.

226

The emeralds flip out of the crown. Rather strangely, both have flat backs, but when you hold them together you see why: they are two halves of the same huge stone. Congratulating yourself on your acquisition you secrete them in your rucksack and move on. Make a note of your find on your *Adventure Sheet* and turn to 78.

227

Katya leaps behind the rocks and scrambles out of sight, and you are not far behind. The riders thunder up to where you are hiding. Both of you freeze, but then Katya glimpses something and screams: 'Caarth!' Surely not! The dreaded Snakemen of the Desert of Skulls *can't* be raiding this far east! Katya springs up, her sword already in her hand, as the riders turn and gallop towards you. You stand too, ready for battle. Turn to 247.

228

The two gems slot into the hilt perfectly, and power courses through your veins! The emerald Eyes of Telak gleam with holy energy. Waving the sword above your head, you cry, 'Telak be with me!' and leap for Laskar. Turn to 400.

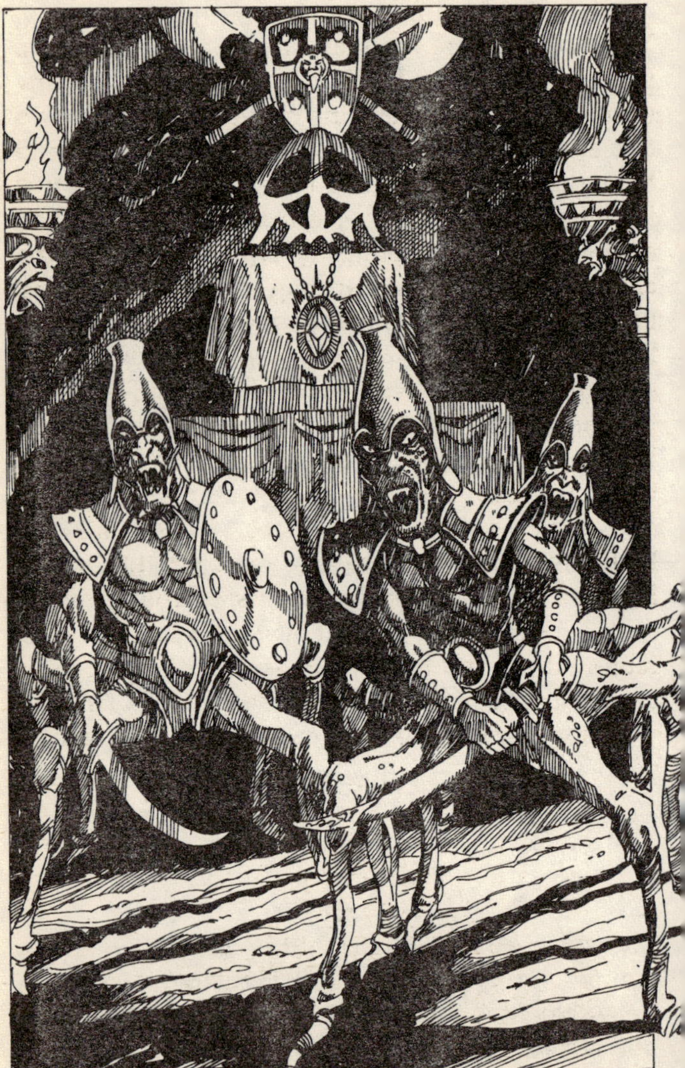

229

You pause before the magnificent altar, offering a prayer of thanks to Telak. The jewel is a huge ruby suspended from a glittering chain, and resting on a carved plinth. The piece is exquisite; how it could have remained untouched here in this place of Evil is a miracle. You gaze deep into the ruby, marvelling at the fire that flickers at its heart. And then the clicking starts, like the tapping of a huddle of blind beggars, like the creaking of a windmill in a gale. From both sides it comes – and something, no some *things* – are moving in the shadows. Then the – the *things* step out from the shadows, in all their insane glory. Skeletal, spider-like bodies are topped by bizarre travesties of human features, long dead and long enslaved by Chaos. These are the Ishkarim, demonic guardians created by the Demon Lords to watch over their most important treasures. As the ice-cold gaze of their dead eyes takes in your features you shudder, your heart sinking in your chest. But still, if you have come this far . . . Are you wearing a priest's robe (turn to **15**) or not (turn to **70**)?

230

You hurry away before the Orcs can react, slipping through the trees and bushes. You run and run, putting a great distance between yourself and the grotesque funeral. When you reach the far end of the woods you pause for a moment and stand there, panting. Suddenly your ears prick up, as they pick up the sound of horse's hoofs, coming closer. Turn to **185**.

231

A giant Running Lizard snarls down at you, a heavily armoured Lizard Man perched in a saddle on its back is poking at you with a javelin.

RUNNING LIZARD   SKILL 7   STAMINA 8

For every round of combat you fight, roll one die. If you roll 1, the rider manages to hit you with his javelin. Deduct 1 STAMINA point. If you kill the Lizard, turn to **104**.

232

'In the name of Alexandros the Second, my father, and in the name of Alexandros the First, my sacred forefather, I command you to be gone!' you shout into the wind. Nothing happens for a long moment, and then the noise of battle begins to fade. A ghostly warrior materializes before you.

'Forgive us. For many long years we have awaited the command of a captain from Vymorna so that we may turn to our rest. We hear now and obey at last. Our battles are over.' The spirit salutes you and fades slowly away into the mist. You shudder, waiting for your nerves to calm, before moving on and marching east. The sun finally breaks through the mist and soon the sky is clear. You pause at noon to eat some Provisions (deduct 1 meal from your *Adventure Sheet*). Turn to **257**.

233

You are pushed out of White-eye's caravan into the darkness, and spend an uncomfortable night huddled under a bush. Next morning the caravan is gone, though you didn't hear it leaving. You move on, hacking your way east into the jungle. It's very hot and humid, and by noon you are sweating like a pig on a spit-roast. Turn to **204**.

234

You come to the front of a large ruined warehouse. Quickly, will you run around the building to the right (turn to **266**), to the left (turn to **178**), or will you enter the building (turn to **159**)?

235

Roll two dice. If you roll less than or equal to your SKILL score, turn to **25**. If you roll higher than your SKILL score, turn to **291**.

236

During the night you wake, and for a moment wonder where you are. In the dull glow of the dying fire you can see Laskar crouched cross-legged, muttering and swaying. You can't hear any words, but it looks as though he is praying. You lie back and slip once more into sleep. Turn to **190**.

237

Sneaking around the pen between the fence and some ramshackle tents, you come across a small Lizard Man sitting near a tethered Pterodactyl, snoozing in the hot sun. Obviously the pilot of the beast, he is dressed in supple leathers and wears a peculiar hat like a skull-cap on his head. You must creep past him if you are to continue. Roll two dice. If you roll less than or equal to your SKILL score, turn to **121**. If you roll higher than your SKILL score, turn to **37**.

238

Each of the three boats – narrow, sleek and low in the water – carries two Swamp Goblins. Small darts from their blow-pipes start to fall in the water around you. You can take evasive action (turn to **40**); shoot at them from a distance with your bow, if you have one (turn to **212**), or sail right at them and prepare to attack (turn to **109**).

239

You pull yourself over the edge of the escarpment, to find yourself staring into the lively eyes of a wizened old man. You flinch back as he pushes his staff towards you, then grin and use it to pull yourself up. 'Laskar?' you ask.

'The same. Welcome, I have been expecting you.' The man is very old and looks shabby, but sprightly and quick-witted. He leads you up the rocky hillside to a large and very cosy cavern. Over a tasty rock-rabbit stew he tells you how he knows of you. 'My – or should I say our – master came to me in a vision three nights ago, though he is hard-pressed, and bade me aid you in your quest. This I willingly do. In the morning we have much to do, so for now you should take as much rest as you can.' He refuses to answer any questions tonight, and commands you to sleep. Eventually you give in and do so. Turn to **236**.

240

Make a note on your *Adventure Sheet* of how many of the eight Lizard Men escaped you. 'They'll be back with reinforcements,' says the man, as you watch them ride away.

'That's all very well,' you reply, 'but who on Titan *are* you?' He introduces himself as 'the one and only' Julius Lecarte, adventurer and trader, roaming Southern Allansia with Snag, his pet Sabre-toothed Tiger, in search of his explorer father, Tadeus, who disappeared several years ago. You haven't heard of his father, you tell him, but go on to relate the tale of your adventures so far. 'We should really head for Capra, about half a dozen leagues from here,' he tells you. 'They're holding out against the raiders for now and they're still able to provide a safe haven for a fugitive. When Vymorna falls, though, it'll take all of the Axehead Plains with it, worse luck. Now, about these Lizard Men of yours . . .' Turn to **79**.

241

The Goblins are well behind you but the river is now rough with white-water rapids, which are making headway difficult. Will you keep going (turn to **364**), or pull over to the bank (turn to **317**)?

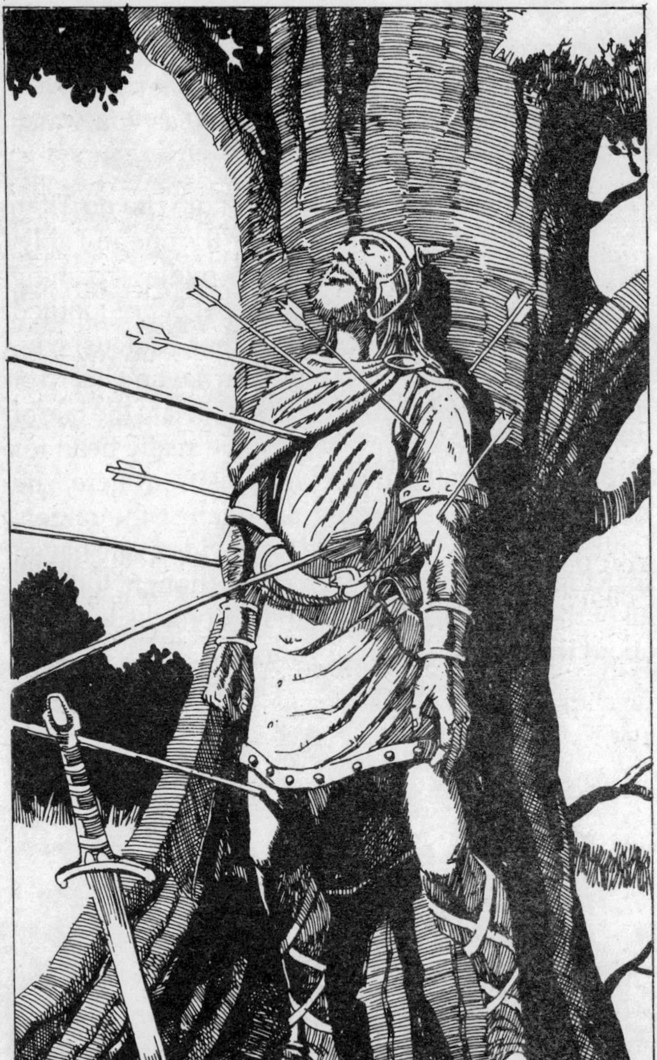

242

You creep carefully between the trees to where the birds were wheeling. Ugh! Up ahead is a most grisly sight. The body of a lightly armoured warrior, obviously an explorer or adventurer, is pinned to the trunk of a tree by arrows and spears. Worse, his chest has been slashed by a huge set of claws that could only belong to something like a very large tiger! The explorer's pack holds some dried rations, which count as 2 Provisions and which you may take with you if you wish (make a note on your *Adventure Sheet* if you decide to do so). After all, you morbidly reflect, he won't be needing them where he's gone. Turn to **80**.

243

You pull yourself up into the tree. There's a small hollow in the branches, and lying in it is a large man-sized bundle wrapped up in leaves and vines. Will you investigate this strange object (turn to **394**), or climb back down and take the bridge (turn to **199**)?

244

The passageway narrows until it is just wide enough for you to squeeze down. The smooth walls turn rough and you seem to be heading deep into the mountainside! Suddenly the tunnel stops in a small, dusty chamber. There is nothing in the chamber, and no exits lead from it. Thank Telak you weren't trapped in here by the Lizard Men. You shudder, and squeeze your way back to the junction to take the other way. Turn to **395**.

245

The sun scorches your neck and arms again as you cut your path away from the temple, glad that you brought your trusty hunting-knife with you. Turn to **204**.

246

The door creaks open after a lot of pushing to reveal a small, rubble-strewn corridor, which leads off into the darkness. Will you go on (turn to **276**), or retrace your steps and explore behind the curtain (turn to **14**)?

247

The riders throw back their hoods and you gasp in amazement. They are Snakemen, cruel raiders from the western desert lands! Katya faints clean away, her fears confirmed. You prepare to fight them but there's no contest against four such warriors. They stake you and the prone body of Katya out in the sun and ride away, never having said a word. The hot sun rises higher and higher in the sky. After only a few minutes, you are desperate for shade and water. For a while you manage to croak some feeble cries for help, but soon your throat is so dry no sound comes. The hours go by. Night comes and goes. Around noon on the fourth day Katya dies. *Test your Luck*. If you are Lucky, turn to **156**. If you are Unlucky, turn to **72**.

248

Laskar grabs the bundle from you and unwraps it, his eyes lighting up greedily. 'Now, you innocent fool! Do you have the Eyes too?' demands the old hermit in a crazed voice. You reach into your pack and retrieve whatever gemstones you found on your travels. (If you have no gems, turn to **57**.) With a disdainful gesture you scatter them across the floor. Laskar dives for them with a mad shout and you lash out at him. Roll two dice. If you roll higher than your SKILL score, turn to **57**. If you roll less than or equal to your SKILL score, turn to **46**.

249

'Some very rare black lotus,' you declare solemnly. He looks at you, then at the lotus, then back at you, then erupts in a fit of giggling. He reaches behind him and opens a large sack to reveal it absolutely brimming with black lotus flowers!

'I'm sorry. It may be worth a king's ransom in the frozen north, but here it's more plentiful than grass, and I have enough to beautify the ugly girls of half a continent!' Turn to **11** and choose again.

250

Test your Luck. If you are Lucky, turn to **325**. If you are Unlucky, turn to **66**.

251

The sun rises, but the mist remains, hanging languidly in the damp air. It is very, very quiet, and rather spooky. Will you keep heading east (turn to **354**), or go north instead (turn to **300**)?

252

The Black Panther flops down on to the branch like a city cat wanting to be stroked, only an arm's length from you, and proceeds to rip apart and eat the deer. You shiver in the darkness, hardly daring to breathe, as it crunches and hacks at the carcass with worrying dexterity. After two hours or so, the great beast stands and tidily pushes the bones of its meal off the branch. It stretches, arching its back, and strides off into the darkness. As it reaches the edge of the moonlight, though, it turns and sniffs the air, and stares right at where you are hiding. It fixes your eyes with its own, blinks once, nods its head slightly, and then leaps away into the night. You have had a lucky escape. Should you ever encounter a creature with such eyes again you may turn, if you wish, to paragraph **142** instead of to those to which you are directed. Make a note of that number on your *Adventure Sheet*, and then turn to **44**.

253

You hurry back up the narrow passageway to the chamber with the stairs. Pausing just a moment to get your breath back, you head on up the stairs. Turn to **301**.

254

You jabber something along the lines of, 'Oh, my lady, your most humble servant apologizes for his rude intrusion!' Bowing low before the astonished creature, you step backwards, making to leave the tent. *Test your Luck*. If you are Lucky, you leave the tent safely (turn to **319**). If you are Unlucky, she reacts angrily and attacks you (turn to **149**).

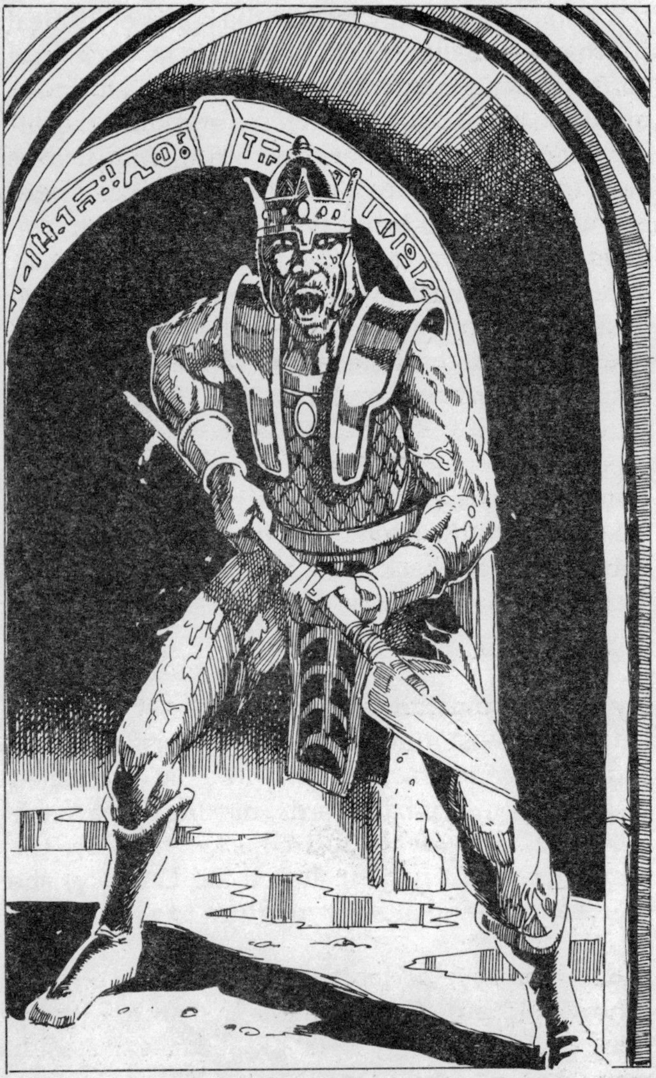

255

A set of crumbling steps leads up to a large door marked with strange, arcane symbols. You listen carefully at the door and hear a sound like metal coins being rubbed together. You ready your sword, take a deep breath, and kick the door. There is a massive thump, but the door remains closed. From inside the room comes a crashing sound. You kick the door again and again, but nothing will budge it. Then, to your horror, the door is flung open with a resounding crash. There, in front of you, is a terrifying sight. Framed in the doorway stands a Warrior-king from lost ages past. He has been dead a long time, but something has resurrected him and set him to guard this ancient room. He carries a long javelin, poised ready to thrust at you, and on his head sits a jagged crown studded with emeralds. You must fight him.

WARRIOR-KING   SKILL 10   STAMINA 11

If you defeat this ancient hero, turn to **326**.

256

'Aha!' White-eye declares. 'Now this *is* interesting! Who would ever have thought that such a pretty thing could be made of lead? Yes, I'll take this, with many thanks.' Turn to **191**.

257

You trudge on. Every few seconds, it seems, you wipe the perspiration from your forehead, but a few moments later it is back. The ground slowly rises, becoming rougher and more broken. After a while you are having to scramble around large boulders and clamber up steep inclines. From ahead of you there sounds the bellowing roar of some large beast. You have no choice but to journey on. Unexpectedly you find yourself at the top of a rise; the ground slants sharply down into a depression. And down there, grazing, is a Triceratops, a truly enormous three-horned armoured dinosaur. You can't really hope to sneak past it, surely, but perhaps you would like to try (turn to **207**)? Or maybe you would rather walk along the ridge in search of a detour (turn to **327**)?

258

The rubble gives way and you are falling. In a panic you grab out and manage to connect with a slat of wood hanging over the edge. And then that gives way and you fall to your doom.

259

As it loses the evil spark that animated it, the ancient body crumples to the floor, shattering into fragments of brown dust. All that is left is a rusting suit of antique armour and a tarnished crown holding two emeralds. Do you prise out the gemstones (turn to **197**), or would you rather leave and continue your exploration (turn to **310**)?

260

At the last minute, the beast shies nervously away, rearing up in fright. Unused to such an action, you fall backwards from the saddle and land heavily, the wind knocked out of you. You look up into a forest of spear- and sword-points, and you know the Lizard Men will not accept your surrender. Your quest is at an end before it ever really started.

261

You push through the ruined doors of a huge warehouse – and immediately regret it! The floor of the building is swarming with rats: huge, black, shabby Wharf Rats, which are making short work of a stray dog. Will you fight your way through them (turn to 315), or try to escape (turn to 126)?

262

Your heart sinks as you watch the arrow fall short and land harmlessly in some bushes. There is no time to prepare and fire another one. Desperate action is called for. Will you run forward to light the trap with a taper (turn to 214), or try to flee the copse on foot (turn to 340)?

263

With a victorious shout you burst free of the enemy lines and run off towards the open plains. A few Lizard Men and Trolls give chase, but they are swiftly caught and dealt with by your fellows. As you sprint away, you hear their war-cries spurring you on. Add 1 LUCK point and turn to 53.

264

You glance about frantically, the footsteps making you panicky and confused. There is nowhere to hide in here . . . and then you see it, a large metal ring with a key attached to it, lying half-hidden amid some dusty trash a few paces away. You grab it, fumble with the lock, and then it's open! You escape. Turn to **216**.

265

This Orc is huge, brown-skinned and brawny. What's more, the shaman is so angry at having a 'yooman' at his ceremony that he joins in too! The other Orcs are too drunk to join in, but you must fight these two.

	SKILL	STAMINA
ANGRY ORC	6	9
SEETHING SHAMAN	6	5

If you somehow defeat the two livid humanoids, turn to **230**.

266

You flatten against the wall, but from behind you there comes a clattering sound. The two Orcs are upon you! You must fight both of them at once.

	SKILL	STAMINA
First MARSH ORC	6	7
Second MARSH ORC	6	6

If you defeat them both, turn to **379**.

267

The slope turns into steep steps. With your sword in one hand and your lantern in the other, arms outstretched for balance, you carefully clamber down the twisting steps until you reach a fair-sized chamber. Its walls are carved with intricate patterns, which seem to detail legendary events from ancient history. There is also a small altar, decorated with sunbeams and other symbols of the sun goddess. The room is littered with debris and dust, but apart from the odd spider weaving yet another cobweb there is nothing of interest to you here. There are two exits from this room: a wide archway covered by a large rotting curtain (turn to **14**), and a small metal-bound door, which hangs half off its hinges, to your right (turn to **246**).

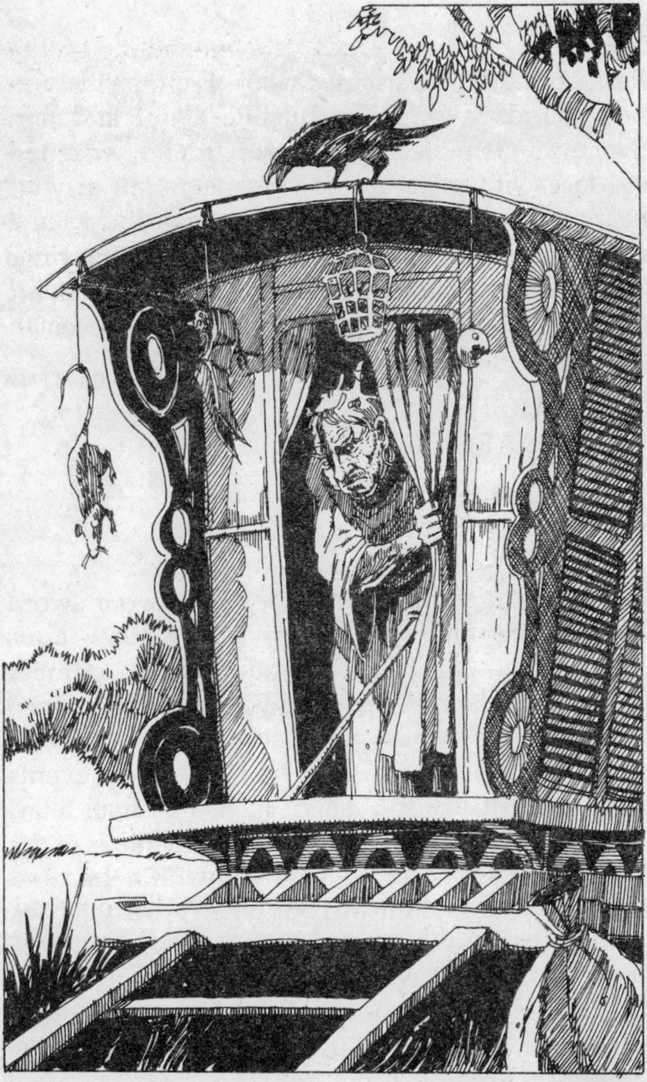

268

You creep up to the gaudy caravan and rap on the frame beside the curtained door. From inside you hear sounds of something bustling about, and then the curtain is pulled back. A very brown, wizened old face with milky-white eyes peers out at you, bearing a welcoming grin. The old man snorts in a peculiar fashion, and beckons you to enter, saying, 'Ah, there you are! Come in! Come in! Don't stand out there all day!' Surprised, you climb the small steps and enter. Turn to **61**.

269

The statues are finally shattered and smashed – but at quite a high cost to your sword, which is notched and blunted. Reduce your Attack Strength by 1. You listen at the door, and hear creaking, like a door blowing in the wind. You listen again, but the noise has stopped. Gripping your sword, you push open the door. Turn to **153**.

270

The wind whistles about you, but all you can think of is the pair of gigantic claws digging into your shoulders. The smell is pretty foul, too, like the inside of a hen-house. And then the claws open, and you are falling. *Test your Luck*. If you are Lucky, turn to **131**. If you are Unlucky, you fall, fall, fall. Your adventure is over before it ever really began.

271

The passage is buckled and twisted, leading away for a short distance before it forks to the left. Straight ahead, the passage narrows and a thin set of steps twists up. The left-hand passage is littered with fallen rocks, but levels off after only a few paces. Will you continue ahead (turn to **154**) or fork left (turn to **353**)?

272

The land is rough and hilly, and the weather very warm, but Katya, your travelling companion, is cheering you up with her talk of life in Coppertown and the northern parts of the Axehead Plains. As you ride, you gaze out over the baking land. Away to the north a small dust cloud is getting larger by the minute. Someone – or something – is riding towards you at high speed. Katya hasn't met anyone on the road for two days, and doesn't know who it could be. Will you keep to your path (turn to **176**) or find somewhere to hide before the riders arrive (turn to **227**)?

273

The Black Panther sees you, snarls, and the moonlight glints on its claws as it leaps at you.

BLACK PANTHER   SKILL 10   STAMINA 10

If you defeat the great beast, turn to 44.

274

You carefully pull open one of the towering double doors and slip through. A wide corridor leads away into the darkness, twisted at such an angle that you have great trouble walking along it. It is also littered with rubble, and the left-hand wall looks very unsafe. The passage turns right after twenty paces or so, and down some well-worn steps. You creep down carefully, managing to avoid the worst rubble. Now you come to a T-junction. Will you take the left passage (turn to 312) or the right (turn to 196)?

275

You have been so busy fighting off the Swamp Goblins that you have failed to notice the white waves, which you are now fighting to row against. You have come to an area of white-water rapids, where many keel-splitting rocks lurk just beneath the surface. Will you push harder against the flow and continue up-stream (turn to 364), or steer a tack for the side (turn to 317)?

276

And then . . . *Test your Luck*. If you are Lucky, turn to **281**. If you are Unlucky, turn to **304**.

277

The trenches divide again. To the right there are signs that it is a new construction, for the earth is fresh and dark. The noise of battle is getting closer. Will you take the right (turn to **123**) or the left trench (turn to **18**)?

278

You hack down a large bundle of branches and wide leaves, and lay them out like a mat on the damp ground. As you work, the sun sets and the cool jungle dusk is suddenly upon you. As darkness falls, the only sound you can hear is the lapping of the water just an arm's length away. And then, from the water . . . Turn to **372**.

279

You find some fleshy orange and yellow fruits that prove edible (you may replenish up to 2 Provisions). While you are picking them, you also happen across a very beautiful flower – a black lotus, long fabled for its scent and rarity. If you wish, you may pick it and take it with you before returning to the path. Turn to **257**.

280

The repulsive body of the Lizard Woman crashes into her fragrant mud-bath. You gaze around the tent. It is decorated in appalling taste, but sitting on an occasional table constructed from an enormous crocodile skull is a small pot bearing the legend 'Black Lotus from Kaynlesh-Ma'. You may take it, if you wish (note it on your *Adventure Sheet*). Turn to **319**.

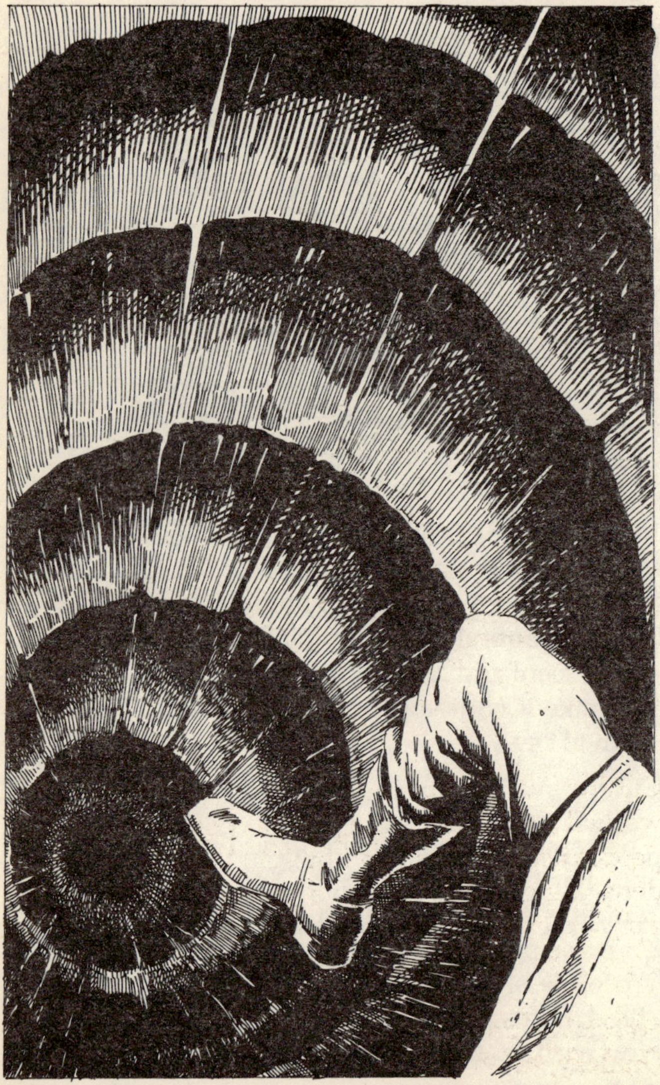

281

Just in time, you stop yourself from falling as the floor gives way to reveal a deep hole, an old well, perhaps. Rubble bounces down into the measureless depths. You could retrace your steps and leave the larger room by the other exit (turn to **14**). Otherwise you must jump the well. Roll two dice. If you roll higher than your SKILL score, turn to **334**. If you roll less than or equal to your SKILL score, turn to **95**.

282

Cutting away the plants, you find a pile of smooth, worked stones. No, not a pile – a wall. It seems that people actually lived and built in the midst of this dense jungle. Will you investigate further (turn to **342**), or set off again on your journey (turn to **97**)?

283

Test your Luck. If you are Lucky, turn to **83**. If you are Unlucky, turn to **157**.

284

You and the strange man set an ambush for the eight Lizard Men pursuing you. You may use as many arrows as you have left and kill one Lizard Man with each arrow. Your companion picks off two more with his arrows. Then, from the low branch of a nearby tree, the Sabre-toothed Tiger leaps down at the inhuman enemy. The mounts of the remaining Lizard Men shy away, turn and flee. Snag chases after them for a while without catching any, then gives up and returns to the scene of the battle. It sniffs the Lizard Man corpses for a moment before turning up its nose and trotting back to its master. Turn to **240**.

285

White-eye simply steps back from you and makes a weird clicking noise with his tongue. From the flickering candles in every corner of the room flames shoot towards the ceiling and coalesce into a glowing light, which flows around your head. A screaming whistle grows in your head as the Guardian Spirit engages you in mind combat.

GUARDIAN SPIRIT   STAMINA 16

Fight as normal, but instead of comparing SKILL with one die roll, the opponents in a mental fight roll two dice and add the result to their STAMINA score to find their Mental Attack Strength. The opponent with the lower score loses two STAMINA points as in a normal fight. If you defeat the Guardian Spirit it will fade away into nothingness. Turn to 328.

286

The rubble gives way beneath your feet and suddenly you are falling into a hole. You flail about in panic, and manage to catch hold of a plank of wood hanging from the side – which gives way, and you plummet down the ancient well to your doom.

287

The foul, alcohol-sodden Orcs greet you as one of their own, giving you plenty of smelly hugs and prods. None of them seems to be in any state to realize that you are in disguise. One very deaf old Orc leans over to you and bellows in your ear. ''Oose sprogling are yoo, then? I naint seen yoo before!' The party goes deathly quiet. Who will you say you are:

Your real name?	Turn to 66
Shagbad, child of Skurfric?	Turn to 360
Ugrat, child of Kuzbag?	Turn to 163

288

With a shock of impact that sets your arm ringing, a massive Cave Troll in Lizard Man livery careers into you, stopping you in your tracks. Battle is joined.

CAVE TROLL   SKILL 9   STAMINA 9

If you defeat this powerful enemy, turn to **23**.

289

Immediately it is very cool – and very dark. You light your lantern and peer about you. The passage is decorated with rows of statues, now toppled and smashed. The floor beneath your feet may once have been a flight of steps, worn smooth to a shallow slope, which climbs down into another covered courtyard. From here lead off two passages, both dark and uninviting. Will you take the one to the right (turn to **171**) or to the left (turn to **267**)?

290

The ground becomes more rolling and grassy. You leap a small rocky stream and bound off towards a copse. Would you rather avoid the trees (turn to **201**) or head straight for them (turn to **303**)?

291

The web twists tighter and tighter around you until you are completely immobile. The only parts you can move are your eyes, which slowly widen in sheer terror as the Wasp Spider begins to feed. Your adventure ends here.

292

You grab your rucksack, dive for the liana, swing down and hit the ground at a run, expecting every moment to feel the dull thud of arrows into your back. There are howls of anger but nothing follows you. By mid-afternoon, when you stop to pick more fruit for your Provisions, you are well away from the area. You are annoyed that your rucksack is empty, but at least you have something to carry your supplies in (cross off everything except your sword, knife and rucksack from your *Adventure Sheet*). While you are eating, you hear a loud flapping coming from through the trees. *Test your Luck*. If you are Lucky, turn to **186**. If you are Unlucky, turn to **99**.

293

The ruby slips into the hilt of your sword, glowing dully in the semi-darkness. With a howl for vengeance you leap for Laskar. The old man looks momentarily horrified, but parries your blow easily with his staff! Where is the fabled power of the weapon? An arrow thumps into your shoulder, another into your leg. You drop to the ground and the Lizard Men close in, swords raised for their final blows. Your quest is at an end.

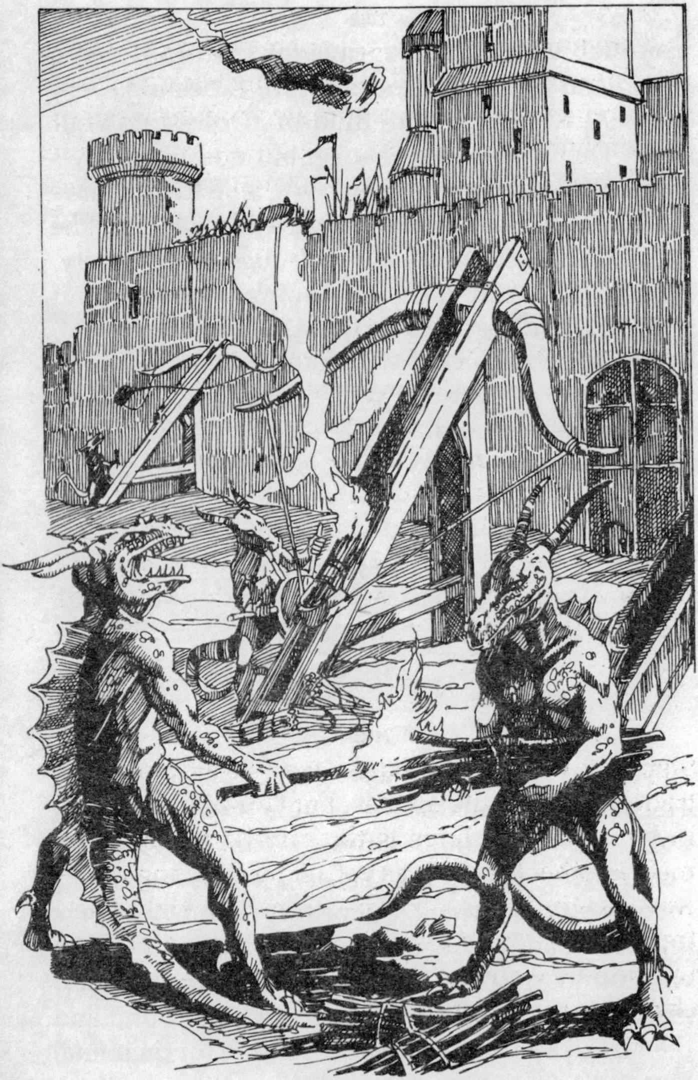

294

You are now deep inside the enemy camp, and you must be even more vigilant. Looking back, you can see a tremendous battle raging away on the western side of Vymorna. Close by, though, a large catapult is bombarding the city with blazing bales. Will you sneak on (turn to **363**), or try to find some way to put this siege engine out of action (turn to **116**)?

295

Suddenly an angry shout comes from the direction of the north bank and instinctively you dive for the bottom of the boat. Arrows thud into the wood. Roll one die. If you roll 1–2 you are hit by an arrow: deduct 2 STAMINA points. By the time you peer out again your boat has floated past the danger. In the centre of the river a huge galley sculls by, and disappears into the haze again. Thanking your stars that you chose to hug the bank, you row on. Turn to **376**.

296

Stepping over fresh bodies, you sneak along the trenches. The route divides, but you keep on heading in what you hope is the same direction. You meet another junction; as you stand deciding which way to go, a noise comes from the right-hand trench. Will you stay back in the shadows and listen to find out who it is (turn to **338**), or leap out and challenge them (turn to **43**)?

297

You step into the next chamber – and find more of the same: rows and rows of bodies, all neatly arranged in racks. Your nerves begin to ache with the effort of remaining calm as you carefully tiptoe through into the third chamber. Here some upheaval has thrown rotting corpses and bare skeletons across the floor, where they lie in a grotesque tangle. Shuddering, you pick your way across the room. Turn to **323**.

298

Your arms are strong and manage to pull your boat clear of the current. You beach the small craft against the north shore and remove all your equipment. You may stop here and eat some Provisions while you take in your surroundings. You are on the edge of the jungle: you may either plunge straight into the jungle and head east (turn to **175**), or you could head north along the fringes of the jungle before turning east further on (turn to **27**).

299

'Telaakk! Teellaaaaaghkk!' echoes back at you, but in voices tinged with sardonic laughter. 'Courage! Swords! Pride! All bring DEAAATHHHHH!' Turn to **7**.

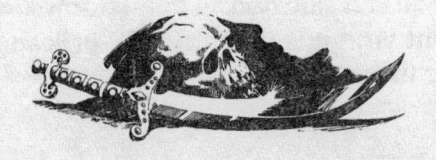

300

The country north of Capra is gently rolling downs, but a deep, morning mist hides most of it. It is cool, and just a tinge spooky, too! Still, in the quiet you should be able to hear anyone approaching you. You trudge north. By mid-morning the mist still shows no sign of lifting. And then, from up ahead, a bell starts to toll. You pause, thinking you imagined it. No, there it goes again! That's funny, you think, no one in Capra mentioned any settlements along this route. You decide to investigate. Are you in disguise (turn to **122**) or not (turn to **369**)?

301

The staircase spirals on up, though thankfully its condition is not too bad. Eventually, after a taxing climb, you reach the top, where your way is barred by another small metal-bound door. You sneak through, into a dingy anteroom. Through an archway you can see into the temple. Laskar is standing, his back towards you, as if contemplating the small altar before him. Will you enter and join him (turn to **217**) or wait a moment so as not to disturb him (turn to **140**)?

302

As the horse reaches your tree, you leap out with a cry. It is a woman, obviously human, and dressed in a dusty messenger's uniform. She is startled, and goes to draw her sword. Will you attack her (turn to **384**) or lower your weapon and greet her (turn to **396**)?

303

You are nearly at the copse, and you seem to be escaping from your pursuers. And then, against all the odds, there's the rush of an arrow from the trees and your mount falls from under you! You tumble to the ground, cursing your luck. A man appears from behind a tree, a bow in his hand, and peers at you as if working out whether or not you survived. You pick yourself up and dust yourself down, unable to believe what has happened! Will you stand to face the Lizard Men (turn to **189**) or run for the trees (turn to **209**)?

304

The rubble gives way and suddenly you fall into a hole that has opened up beneath your feet. You flail wildly and manage to catch hold of a plank of wood hanging from the side. Then that gives way and you fall down the ancient well . . . to your doom.

305

You turn round and head back in what you are certain is the direction of Capra. The mist is very confusing, though, and you are not at all sure that you are going in the right direction. The howling starts again, this time to the south of you, though you cannot decide how far away. Every part of you is saying 'RUN!' and you are barely controlling your fear. Hold it! Haven't you passed those bushes before? Are you walking in circles now? You could continue walking (turn to **102**), or stop here and hope the mist eventually lifts (turn to **398**).

306

Your sword shatters, smashed into several pieces by a vicious blow from your opponent. You reach for the dagger at your belt, but another blow connects with your head. An arrow thuds into your wrist and you drop your dagger. The third blow comes and you fall face down in the blood-red mud.

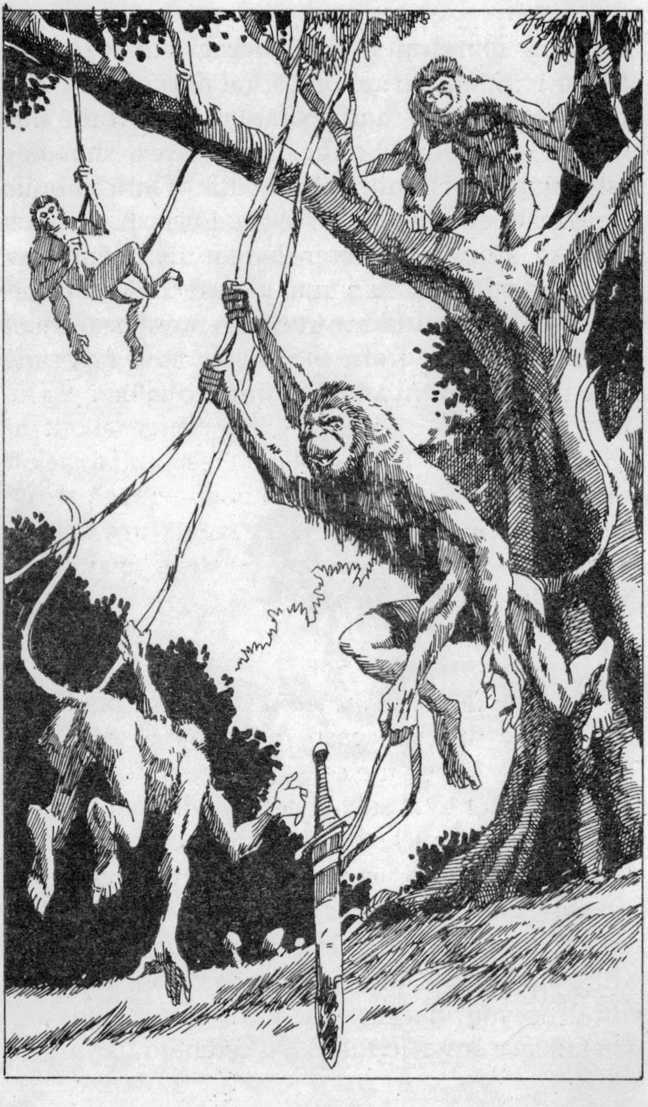

307

The afternoon sun is very warm, but it's quite pleasant in the shade. Just a brief pause, you promise yourself, unbuckling your sword and laying it beside you. You close your eyes. The trees rustle in the breeze, though you don't feel it on your face. You open one eye, to see your sword, still in its scabbard, apparently moving across the grass under its own steam! You spring to your feet. All around you, swinging in the branches, are hordes of small six-limbed monkeys – Krells! As you move they start chattering excitedly, and the noise is deafening! The one dragging away your sword is just about to swing off into the trees. Will you leap and attack it with your knife (turn to **332**), shoot it with an arrow from your father's bow, if you have it (turn to **390**), or simply chase after the creature making a threatening noise (turn to **20**)?

308

The panther-god figurine clunks on to the platform, and all the warriors gasp the same word: 'Sku-Rachi!' They kneel, their heads pressed to the floor in a gesture of total subservience. All, that is, save the priest, who picks up the figurine, examines it closely, and draws his knife. You must fight him, and with your Attack Strength reduced by 2 because you are unarmed.

WARRIOR PRIEST   SKILL 7   STAMINA 6

If you defeat the priest, turn to **336**.

309

As one, the riders throw back their hoods. Snakemen! The legendary rulers of the Desert of Skulls. What are they doing so far east? Four Caarth against one human is no contest, and soon you are feeling their rough scaly hands staking you out under the hot sun. The Snakemen ride away, never having uttered a single word, and leave you to the circling vultures. You lie out under the burning rays of the sun, at first calling weakly for help but soon becoming so parched you cannot utter a word. You feel yourself becoming delirious, but manage a prayer to Telak. *Test your Luck*. If you are Lucky, turn to **156**. If you are Unlucky, you will not survive, and your adventure must end here.

310

You push open the door at the far end of the room, and find yourself looking down a flight of crumbling stairs. You carefully pick your way down, and follow the passage that leads from them to an old and dusty room, again littered with small pieces of rubble from its cracked ceiling and walls. In a far corner, what appears to be a statue or may be a fountain casts grotesque shadows in the lantern-light. You may examine this (turn to **50**), or leave by the dark passage which leads off opposite (turn to **271**).

311

You push away the remains of the door and peer into the room, which is angled so steeply that it is almost completely on its side and is full of statues and idols. They lie piled high, scattered across the floor like bodies in the aftermath of a battle. There is an exit on the far left wall. You may enter the room to which it leads (turn to **138**), or retrace your steps (turn to **353**).

312

After you have gone ten paces or so, the corridor opens out into an almost level-floored chamber only a few paces across. A stone bench is set into the wall on either side of you, and opposite you steps lead down into the darkness. You may rest here and eat some Provisions (check your *Adventure Sheet*), if you wish. Turn to **2**.

313

A guard looks up and sees you. You look back at him, and then you both grab for your weapons and rush to attack!

| LIZARD MAN GUARD | SKILL 8 | STAMINA 9 |

If you defeat him, turn to **181**.

314

Keeping close to the northern shore, you paddle against the gentle current of the slow-moving river. The river-bank is sparsely vegetated at first, but the trees become thicker as you come closer to the jungle. There is no sign of any more Lizard Men, but you keep a wary eye open anyway. Turn to **295**.

315

The Wharf Rats squeak in terror, and scuttle back into the rubble. You are amazed, but you will not stick around for too long in case they come back. Turn to **203**.

316

You hastily dive down behind a convenient pile of barrels. There is a clamour of voices very near by: a high-pitched squeaking and a deep growling, both speaking the guttural Lizard Man language. Will you keep your head down (turn to **134**), or give in to your curiosity and have a peep (turn to **86**)?

317

The current becomes very strong alongside the river-bank, whipping the water into a small whirlpool that threatens to wreck your flimsy craft. Roll two dice. If you roll higher than your SKILL score, turn to **364**. If you roll less than or equal to your SKILL score, turn to **298**.

318

The Pterodactyl plummets to the ground, but unfortunately the Lizard Man leaps clear, and races towards you in anger.

LIZARD MAN SKILL 6 STAMINA 8

If you defeat the Lizard Man, turn to **164**.

319

Shuddering at your close shave, you pick your way through the maze of tents, baggage carts and piles of stores, which make up the Lizard Men's camp. You're nearing its edge and, with luck, will soon be free of the siege. Now if only you had a mount, you could put a great distance between yourself and the enemy in a very short time. Just as you are thinking this, you notice a set of pens up ahead holding a variety of animal mounts! Do you want to investigate further (turn to **148**), or would you rather creep round it (turn to **237**)?

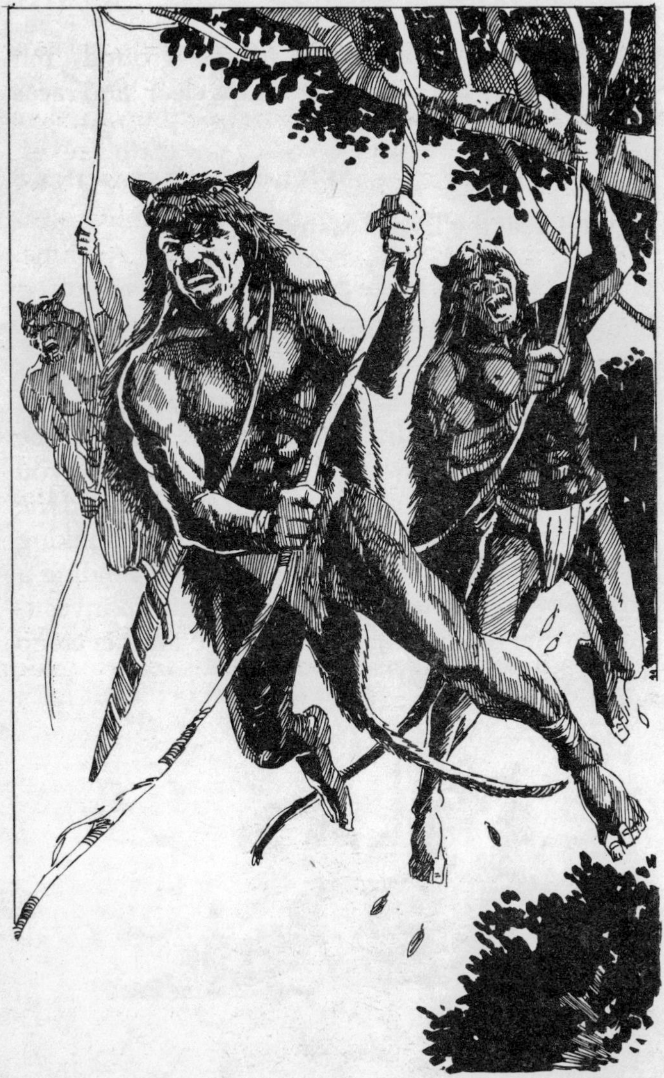

320

With a howl, a band of warriors clad in panther skins swing down at you from the trees, brandishing long knives fashioned like tiger claws. Before you have time to react your arm is nicked by one of the knives. Deduct 2 STAMINA points. You recover, draw your sword, and leap to the attack. There are five warriors in all, and you must fight them two at a time. Each time a warrior falls another takes his place; they all have the same SKILL and STAMINA scores.

PANTHER WARRIORS   each   SKILL 5   STAMINA 6

If you take two consecutive hits or your STAMINA score drops to 4 or less, turn to **381**. If you defeat the warriors, turn to **155**.

321

Roll two dice. If you roll higher than your SKILL score, turn to **90**. If you roll less than or equal to your SKILL score, turn to **216**.

322

Disgustingly deformed, a mutant Lizard Man pulls its stunted, misshapen body from the mud and leaps to the attack!

MUTANT
LIZARD MAN SKILL 6   STAMINA 6

If it scores two consecutive hits against you, turn to **162**. If you score two consecutive hits against it or kill it, roll one die. If you roll 1–2, turn to **208**; 3–4, turn to **192**; 5–6, turn to **172**.

323

You reach the other side of the room, although every moment you expect a ghastly skeletal hand to clutch at you, an animated skull to bite at you! The next chamber is in even worse condition than the last one, with bones and rubble scattered everywhere. There are three exits: an arch to the left (turn to **125**), another arch to the right (turn to **41**), and a small tunnel that leads away directly ahead of where you came in (turn to **67**).

324

The warriors smother you, pushing you to the ground so that they can bind you with tough vines. You are marched through the jungle until you come to a very large tree, whereupon a vine is attached to your waist and you are dragged up into the branches. Despite your initial shock at being so high above the ground, and the obvious danger of your predicament, you are intrigued by the platforms and rope-bridges which the warriors have built up in the tree-tops. A tall, white-haired elder, obviously, from his dress, the high priest or shaman, approaches you and stares deep into your eyes. If you have stared into another creature's eyes recently you will know of a section to turn to. He then takes your rucksack and shakes it out on to the floor and paws through it. Do you have a panther idol? If you do, turn to **308**; if you do not, turn to **75**.

325

No one seems to notice. You make what you think are convincingly disgusting lip-licking noises, and keep your head down as if in deep thought. But now is the time when everyone meets the assembled relatives. Would you rather try to make a break for freedom (turn to **66**), or not (turn to **287**)?

326

As it loses the evil spark that animated it, the ancient body crumples to the floor, shattering into fragments of brown dust. All that is left is a rusting suit of antique armour and a tarnished crown holding two emeralds. You may prise out the gemstones (turn to **226**), or perhaps you would rather leave and continue your exploration (turn to **78**).

327

The ridge circles around the depression, heading for a thick clump of trees. The first trees are young saplings, but soon you come to larger, thick-trunked trees. You brush against one of them, and almost leap out of your skin as it moves and an enormous Tyrannosaurus Rex rises from among the trees! Your heart sinks into your boots. What can you do? Roll two dice. If you roll higher than your SKILL score, you must attack the creature (turn to **132**). If you roll less than or equal to your SKILL score, you may be able to try something else (turn to **81**).

328

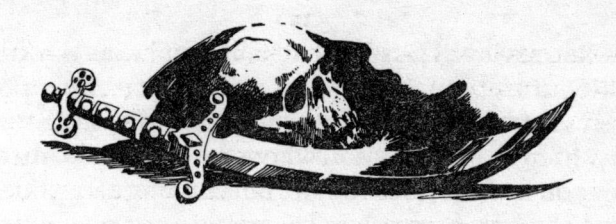

'You hot-headed young fool!' thunders White-eye. 'There was no need for such violence. You have taken something that was mine, and destroyed it, too! Now I claim something of yours in fair exchange. What will you trade me for the life of a living being?' The old man looks so angry you feel desperately ashamed for what you have done, but all you can do is reach into your pack and give him two items, if you have any, or if you have nothing he will accept all your Provisions. 'Now leave immediately!' he rages at you. Deduct 1 LUCK point and turn to **233**.

329

The far corner of the room is crumbled and battered, and a trail of loose dirt shows where the Slug probably entered. You tiptoe round the edge of the rubble, keeping an eye open for a second monster, until you come to the double doors. The Slug has finished the first set of curtains, and is now slithering towards those hanging over the second alcove. Will you attack the creature (turn to **375**) or leave the room to continue your exploration (turn to **274**)?

330

After several hours of hacking your way through the jungle you seem to be making very little progress, and your morale is falling rapidly. Eventually, though, you come to where the land dips. Ahead of you is more thick jungle, but running alongside it is a shallow depression, several leagues long, which is marshy and damp. Will you continue through the jungle (turn to 397) or follow the depression (turn to 117)?

331

The sun is higher in the sky, and you are becoming very weary. You were not cut out for such long treks by your courtly upbringing! You would very much like to stop and rest awhile, but up ahead a scraggy bunch of vultures seems to be circling above something hidden from sight by the trees. Will you see what has attracted their attention (turn to 242) or continue your march (turn to 80)?

332

The Krell swings down into the lower branches, screeching and swiping at you. Two more of the creatures spring down to aid it, and suddenly you have a battle on your hands. You must fight all three at once.

	SKILL	STAMINA
First KRELL	5	4
Second KRELL	6	5
Third KRELL	5	6

If you defeat these three, the rest will run off and you can retrieve your precious sword before moving on. Turn to **221**.

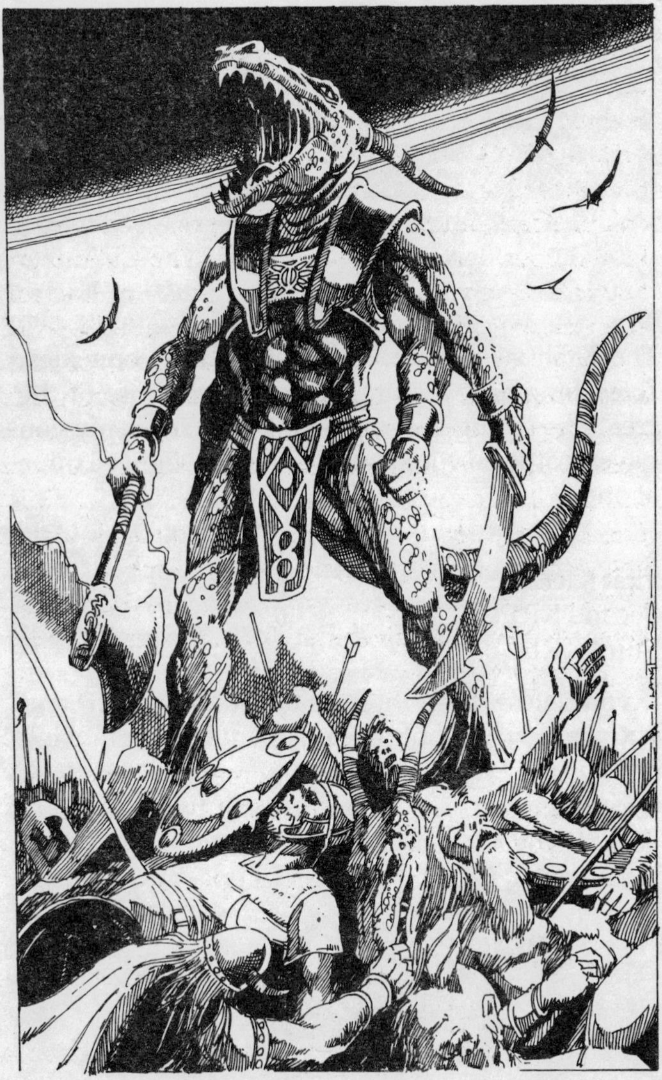

333

And suddenly the roar of battle ceases, and the ranks of warriors part. Atop a mound of human bodies, right at the centre of the fighting, is the Lizard Man Champion. Nearly three metres tall, four-armed and splattered with gore, the immense creature is swinging a barbaric war-axe and a huge knife larger than your own sword. The Champion howls insanely, drunk with blood-lust, calling on any brave warrior to challenge him to a fight. Will you step forward to take him on (turn to **26**), or take advantage of the distraction to break through the lines (turn to **213**)?

334

The rubble gives way and suddenly you fall into the hole. You flail wildly and manage to catch hold of a plank of wood hanging from the side. Then that gives way and you plummet down the ancient well . . . to your doom.

335

The chest rattles – there's something inside it! Examining it closely, you notice it has a Z-shaped lock. If you have a key of that shape, turn to **101**. If you would rather try to smash it open, turn to **127**.

336

You dive for your sword and rucksack, grab a vine and swing down from the platform. You hit the ground running, expecting a hail of darts to thump into your back with every step. However, nothing follows you but a few angry howls and shrieks, and as the ground begins to rise into the foothills of the Lion Heights you feel safe enough to slow your pace to a trot. By mid-afternoon the ground is rising steadily and the trail is becoming steeper. You stop to eat some Provisions in the shade of a large thorn-bush. As you are munching a large, sweet fruit you hear the sound of heavy flapping wings. *Test your Luck*. If you are Lucky, turn to **186**. If you are Unlucky turn to **99**.

337

As the creatures die they fade away into nothing, leaving you alone in the room of statues. You retrieve the jet eyes and your lantern, and leave the room. The passage leads off at a very acute angle, and you find yourself walking more on what used to be the wall than on the floor. Turn to **152**.

338

You hang back in the shadows and watch excitedly as three stooped, hooded figures creep by. Will you attack them (turn to **43**) or wait for them to disappear before taking the right trench (turn to **206**) or the left (turn to **277**)?

339

You manage to evade the boats, but they give chase. Roll one die. If you roll 1–3, you are hit by as many blow-pipe darts. Deduct 1 STAMINA point for each, before you leave the Goblins behind. Turn to **241**.

340

You leap on to the horse and urge it with your spurs to gallop away, but too late: the Lizard Men are upon you! Turn to **36**.

341

As you reach the copse, a hand shoots out and grabs you, whirling you around. A dagger is held to your throat and wild eyes stare into yours. 'Eh? You're human!' The man, dressed in furs and with straggling hair and beard, seems very surprised. 'What you doin' ridin' a lizard? I could've killed you!' You quickly gabble out the story of your escape from the city, and that the Lizard Men are chasing you. The man peers out from behind the tree, taking in the sight of your pursuers, before returning his attention to you. Turn to **21**.

342

You continue to cut a path along the river-bank, finding more traces of what must have been quite a substantial settlement many years ago. You follow the curve of the river for some distance, and then find yourself in a wide grassy clearing. Gazing around, you suddenly realize that you are in the open courtyard of a stone temple, most of which is covered in vines and undergrowth. Large columns lie buried under rampant vegetation, and crumbling stone walls support bushes and small trees. The place is very quiet and feels almost sacred as though it had never lost its spiritual atmosphere. Will you investigate further (turn to **151**) or move on (turn to **245**)?

343

You are summarily searched and trussed up. You still have your trusty hunting-knife tucked into your belt, but you decide to wait for a more opportune time to escape. The funeral continues, and the Orcs start to pass around the Guursh, the skull-splitting Orcish ale, one of the most intoxicating and revolting substances on Titan. Carefully twisting your wrists this way and that, you manage to cut the rope that binds you. *Test your Luck*. If you are Lucky, turn to **230**. If you are Unlucky, you are noticed and must fight the Orcs (turn to **265**).

344

White-eye opens the phial and sniffs the purple liquid. His eyes widen and glaze over; a strange smile crosses his lips as a look of sheer happiness transforms his face. He becomes calm again, shaking his head as if to clear his mind. 'Yes, I will take this. Thank you,' he says. You wonder whether *you* should have tried the stuff before now, but it is too late. Turn to **191**.

345

You stop yourself just in time as the floor gives way to reveal a deep hole, an old well perhaps. Rubble bounces away down into the measureless depths. You could retrace your steps into the room (turn to **153**). Alternatively, you could try to jump. Roll two dice. If you roll higher than your SKILL score, turn to **258**. If you roll less than or equal to your SKILL score, turn to **205**.

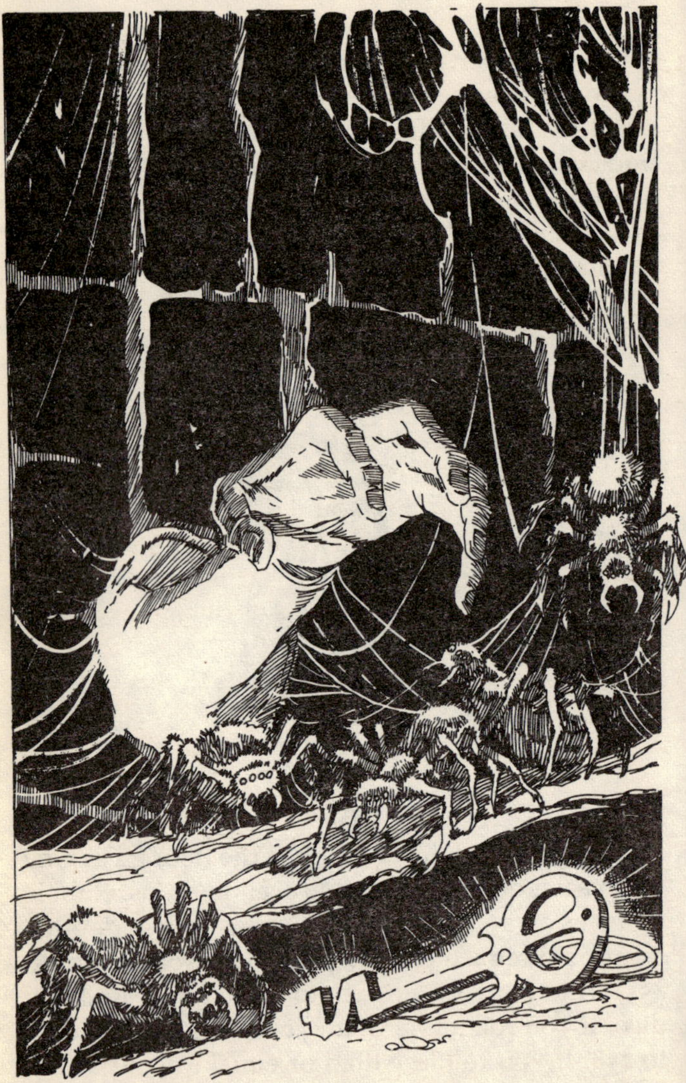

346

Roll one die – as many hairy spiders bit you as the result of your roll when you grabbed for the shiny object. Deduct 1 STAMINA point for each bite. Luckily, though, you had the presence of mind to keep hold of the object as you felt the tiny teeth pricking you. It is a small key, shaped like a Z. You secrete it in your pack; it may come in useful later. Now you may explore the other alcove (turn to **119**) or leave the room (turn to **183**).

347

An arrow whistles past your left ear! Oh, Telak, you think, they're getting close enough to hit me! The ground beneath your mount's sure feet becomes more rolling. As the lizard leaps a small stream you notice a copse just up ahead of you. Will you ride for the copse (turn to **303**), or continue on past it (turn to **201**)?

348

The body of the repulsive creature sinks back into the swamp with a sucking sound, and you spend an uncomfortable night perched too close for comfort to the water's edge. The morning dawns bright and glorious, and you wake face down in the soft mud having succumbed finally to your tiredness, regardless of any danger. For a few moments you wonder why you were afraid to sleep – then the red stain on the surface of the water near by reminds you. You wash, and move on. At least there is no trouble eating in the jungle; you can collect up to your total of 4 Provisions as you walk along. It should just be possible now to see the Lion Heights and Telak's Mount from the top of a tree; you may care to climb up (turn to **393**), or perhaps you would rather continue on your way (turn to **170**).

349

You spend the rest of the afternoon hastily binding branches together to build crude barricades to confuse the riders and direct them into the centre of the copse. Here Lecarte builds a huge bonfire of wood soaked in oil mixed with something he tells you is called, 'Flashpowder: Sulis Vitae from Sardath. Trust me!' As the sun sets you hear galloping hoofs, and a band of warriors on riding lizards thunder out of the dusk. There are all the Lizard Men who escaped, plus a further six – a very large band to be taken on by two adventurers and a Sabre-toothed Tiger! They plunge into the copse towards your light. As the Lizard Men enter one side of the copse, Lecarte and yourself are waiting on the other. Lecarte blows his horn to distract the enemy while you let loose a flaming arrow into the darkness. Roll two dice. If you roll higher than your SKILL score, turn to **262**. If you roll less than or equal to your SKILL score, turn to **16**.

350

But the mounts *are* guarded after all, for as you unhitch one a bell clangs and you hear a shouted challenge! You leap on to the back of the lizard and hare away to the north. Turn to **146**.

351

You nervously peer into an alcove, but find only rotten bones. It is the same story in the next alcove, and the next. If these corpses were buried with any jewels or fabulous treasures they were taken a long time ago, you decide. You will not find Telak's missing parts here. You tiptoe on. Turn to **297**.

352

Heart pounding and lungs bursting through trying not to breathe, you stay as still as you possibly can. The moon slips from behind a cloud and suddenly you can see two eyes, two large cat's eyes. As you get used to the gloom you realize that the beast is an immense Black Panther, dragging a small deer up into the tree to eat! Will you attack it (turn to **273**) or stay as still as you can in the hope that it will go away (turn to **252**)?

353

The high-vaulted corridor leads past murals depicting the many glorious deeds of Telak Swordbearer to a set of wide steps, at the top of which are great double doors, marked with many of Telak's symbols. Carefully, you listen at the doors, but hear nothing. With your sword ready in your hand, you push open one of the doors and step in . . . What a magnificent place! Columns stretch out into the shadows on both sides. The walls are lined with weapons and shields, and carved with murals depicting many great deeds. At their centre stands a magnificent altar to Telak, which bears a small plinth holding the largest ruby you've ever seen! Could *this* be the Eye of Telak? You glance warily around you, peering into the shadows. To one side of the altar there's a small door, obviously leading to the stairs up to where you must meet Laskar. Will you approach the altar (turn to **229**), or leave by the small door (turn to **87**)?

354

You march on, rather enjoying being out in the open countryside despite the sinister mist, which is allowing your imagination to work overtime. The ground is now rolling and grassy, but broken in places by patches of sand and the occasional stream, and dotted with many clumps of thorn-bushes. Suddenly, though, you stop dead as a peculiar howling drifts down to you on the wind. It seems to have come from somewhere up ahead . . . or to your right . . . or to your left. Will you continue on your way (turn to **102**) or retrace your steps (turn to **305**)?

355

You push the door and it gives, but creaks very loudly. In a panic you dive through before the Slug can react, and find yourself slipping down a flight of stone steps just beyond the door. *Test your Luck.* If you are Lucky, turn to **345**. If you are Unlucky, turn to **286**.

356

You cut a track to the river-bank, and wash the sleep and sweat from your face. You check your equipment, and eat some more Provisions. None of the plants around here seems to be edible, but you are guaranteed to find more on your journey. As you are glancing around at the bushes, though, you notice something potentially more interesting: a strange pile of overgrown rocks. Do you investigate (turn to **282**), or set off again on your journey (turn to **97**)?

357

The corridor goes only a short way, leading to a huge brass-bound door. You listen at the door and hear a sound like metal coins being rubbed together. You ready your sword, take a deep breath, and kick the door. There is a massive thump, but the door remains closed. From inside the room comes a crashing sound. You kick the door again, and again, but nothing will budge it. Then to your horror the door is flung open with a resounding crash. There, in front of you, is a terrifying sight. Framed in the doorway stands a Warrior-king from lost ages past. He has been dead a long time, but something has resurrected him and set him to guard this ancient room. He carries a long javelin, poised ready to thrust at you, and on his head sits a jagged crown studded with emeralds. You must fight him.

WARRIOR-KING   SKILL 10   STAMINA 11

If you defeat this ancient hero, turn to **259**.

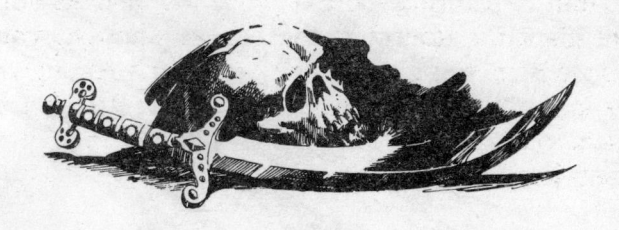

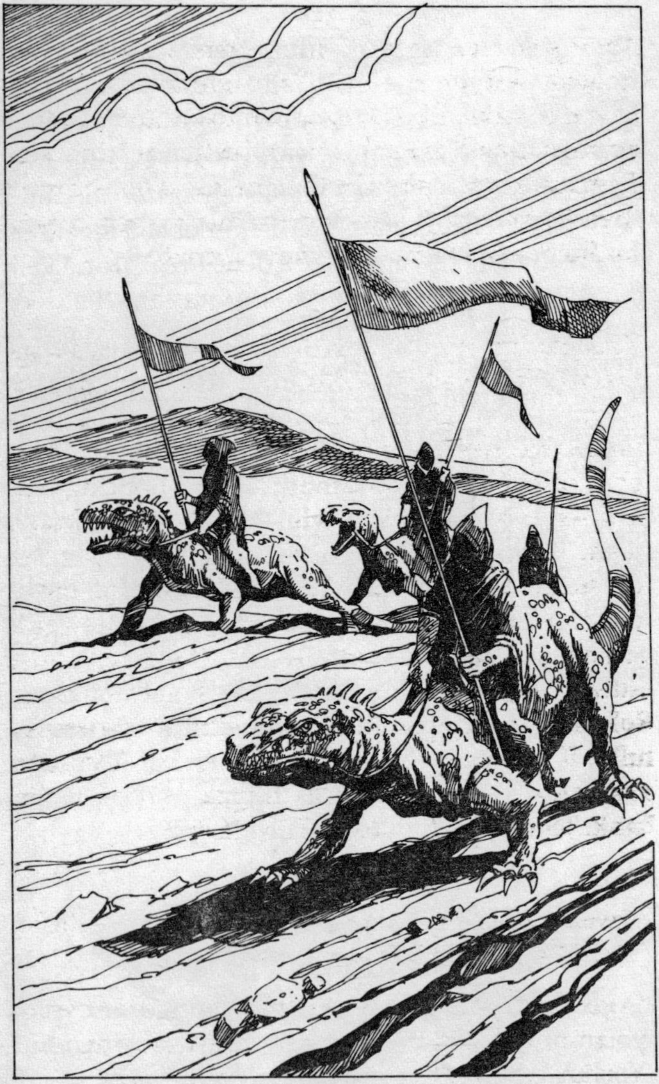

358

Then you see them – four riders, cloaked and hooded despite the heat, and mounted on four-legged lizards. They slow down to a canter as they approach, and stop at a wary distance from you. Their faces are hidden by their hoods. Will you greet them (turn to **383**), attack them (turn to **309**) or wait for them to make the first move (turn to **84**)?

359

You hear the regular splash of many oars as a large Lizard Man galley sculls towards you in midstream. As it approaches your position you duck under the overhanging trees lining the southern bank, and it sails past without anyone noticing you. You let a sigh of relief whistle out through your teeth. Then, out of the corner of your eye, you see the snake. It must have dropped from one of the trees, and now it's slowly slithering its way towards you across the bottom of the boat. You try to lift it out with the flat of your oar before it gets too close. Roll one die. If you roll 1–4, you remove it successfully. If you roll 5–6, it bites your hand. Deduct 1 STAMINA point before it is flipped out on to the bank. Then you paddle on. Turn to **376**.

360

'Never 'eard of yer!' the Orc snarls, peering closer. ''Ere! Youse nain't an Orc, youse a yooman!'

'A *yooman*?' goes the cry. A much younger Orc spins you round, looks at you closely, and draws his club! You have a fight on your hands. Turn to **265**.

361

You have several options as far as routes and your method of travelling are concerned. After long discussions with Vymorna's most learned experts (those who are still alive, at any rate), it was agreed that you could leave the city with a band of warriors who would try to force their way through the enemy lines and enable you to flee from the besieged city on foot, heading north and then east to your goal. Alternatively, you could take the same route but attempt to leave the city in secret, sneaking through the enemy lines just before dawn. Finally, you could sneak down to the docks and attempt to steal a boat, which would take you a fair distance up the River Vymorn before you head east to your goal. Will you try to break out by force (turn to **130**), sneak away before dawn (turn to **93**), or try to steal a boat (turn to **158**)?

362

The revolting corpse flops down, oozing colourless ichor on to the dusty floor. You may now check the first alcove (turn to **68**), the second alcove (turn to **168**), or leave the room (turn to **274**).

363

You hurry along between the tents, keeping your head down. As you come to a well-worn path through the camp, you hear the sound of marching feet coming along it. You must not be caught out here in the open. Will you duck into a tent (turn to **8**) or look for somewhere else to hide (turn to **316**)?

364

The water becomes rougher, and a wave swamps the boat, throwing you overboard. The last thing you remember is the almighty crash of your boat hitting some submerged rocks . . . You wake face down in sand, on the northern bank of the river, with fragments of your ill-fated craft scattered around you. Near by the rapids continue to rage. You get up and check your equipment. Your cloak is in a sorry state and, if you had any Provisions left, they are ruined (cross them off your *Adventure Sheet*), but everything else seems to be intact. You rest while you decide which direction to take. You could head directly east, hacking your way through the jungle until you reach the Lion Heights (turn to **175**), or you could head north along the edge of the jungle before turning east, which would be a longer journey but would mean you spend less time in the jungle (turn to **27**).

365

You must fight the two Marsh Orcs together.

	SKILL	STAMINA
First MARSH ORC	6	7
Second MARSH ORC	6	6

If you defeat them, turn to **379**.

366

You settle behind a tree from where you can see the caravan. Nothing happens, though, and eventually you fall asleep. You awake suddenly to find a wizened old being smiling down at you. You start in fright, but he calms you, saying, 'Come, man-child. Let us go indoors out of the night and find you a better place to sleep!' Intrigued and amazed, you follow him. Turn to **61**.

367

As you wait, plucking up the courage to enter the darkness, you are horrified to see Laskar reach the far side of the ruins – and be surrounded by Lizard Men! The creatures march away with the hermit, and another band has been dispatched in your direction. This is all the incentive you need to duck down into the hole and begin your journey through the darkness. Turn to **289**.

368

The Pterodactyl screeches in panic as it sees its beloved pilot fall to the ground. From away behind you, among the tents, you hear shouts and footsteps. You must get out of here right away. Will you leap on to the back of the Pterodactyl (turn to **387**) or will you try for a riding lizard (turn to **146**)?

369

The ground rises to a small hillock dotted with sparse patches of thorn-bushes and trees. At the crest of the hill a motley group stands gathered around a large funeral bier. Looking closely you can see that, despite the veils and other dark clothes, the mourners are all Orcs! To one side a bizarrely dressed shaman leaps and capers, throwing bones and entrails to the winds in honour of the dead. You could creep closer still and take a better look, or just trek on. While you are deciding, *Test your Luck*. If you are Lucky, turn to **118**. If you are Unlucky, turn to **66**.

370

Roll two dice. If you roll higher than your SKILL score, turn to **291**. If you roll less than or equal to your SKILL score, turn to **3**.

371

The diamond slips into the hilt of your sword, glowing dully in the semi-darkness, With a howl of vengeance you leap for Laskar. The old man looks momentarily horrified, but parries your blow easily with his staff. Where is the fabled power of the sword? An arrow thumps into your shoulder, another into your leg. You drop to the ground and the Lizard Men close in, swords raised for their final blows. Your quest is at an end.

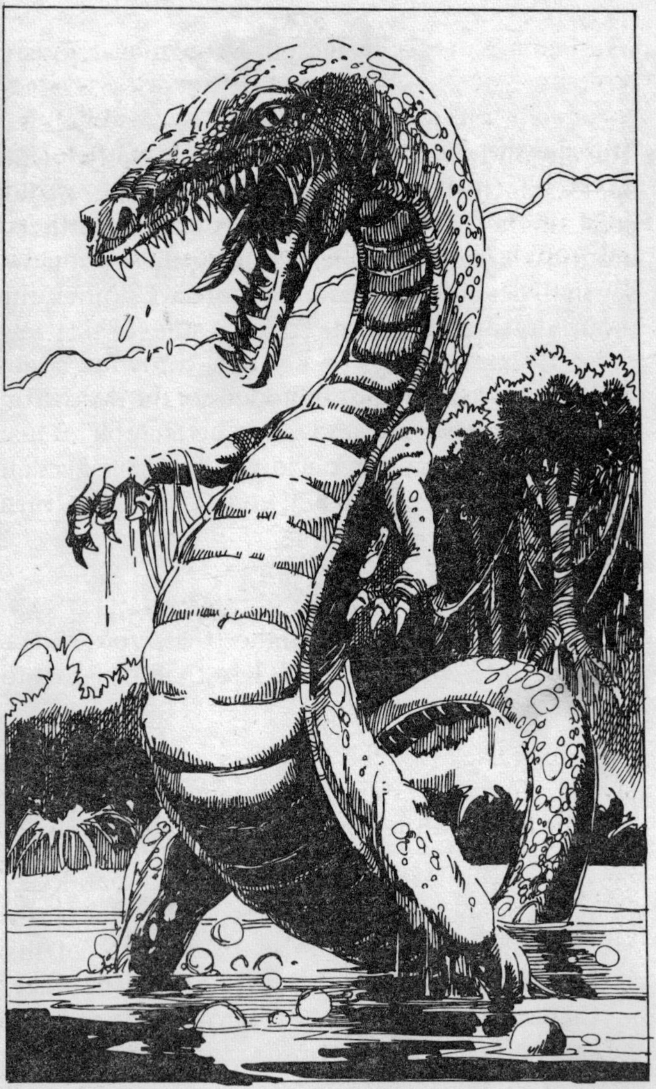

372

And then, from the water, bursts the most repulsive creature you have ever seen. It's a sickly white all over, like the soft underbelly of a crocodile, and indeed the Swamp Mutant shares many of the crocodile's characteristics. It rears up on strong hind legs and snaps at you with a mutated alligator head. All you can do is to bring your sword up to meet its first attack.

SWAMP MUTANT   SKILL 10   STAMINA 16

If you defeat the monstrous creature, turn to **348**.

373

You duck back into the shadows, fumbling for the sword. You are certain that a gemstone should fit into the hilt of the weapon. If you haven't found any gems on your travels, turn to **28**. If you have found some, which will you try to fit into the hilt of the sword, hoping they will be the Eyes of Telak:

The diamond?	Turn to 371
The emeralds?	Turn to 228
The jets?	Turn to 173
The ruby?	Turn to 293

374

You find some fleshy orange and yellow fruits, which prove edible (these count as 2 Provisions). While you are searching about in the undergrowth you also come across a beautiful flower – a black lotus, long fabled for its scent and rarity. You may take it with you, if you wish, before returning to the path and continuing your journey. Turn to **169**.

375

The Giant Slug sees you, and starts to lumber across the rubble towards you. It is a truly repulsive creature, dripping slime and spittle from its mouth as it ripples along. As it is a very slow-moving creature, you may have time to loose an arrow at it. If you have a bow, turn to **224**. Otherwise you will have to fight it using your sword, although, because of its thick skin, your blows will only do it 1 STAMINA point of damage.

GIANT SLUG   SKILL 6   STAMINA 12

If you defeat it, turn to **362**.

376

Giving thanks to Telak for ensuring your safety (though it was a very close shave), you paddle on up-river. The Vymorn sweeps north in a wide, slow-moving curve, and you have no trouble guiding your small craft along. The river curves again, heading east. You paddle along keeping an eye open both sides for any sign of trouble. After an hour or so the river is joined by a tributary flowing from the south; the Lizard River flows from the depths of Silur Cha. As you pass the place where it joins the Vymorn you give thanks that you are not having to go up *that* waterway. It is at this moment that you notice three boats heading towards you from the southern shore. Turn to **238**.

377

The land is rough and hilly, and the weather very warm. You have lost track of the days since you left Vymorna, but pray that your family and friends are holding on. Away to the north a small dust cloud is getting larger by the minute. Someone – or something – is riding towards you at high speed. Will you keep to your path (turn to **358**) or find somewhere to hide before the riders arrive (turn to **139**)?

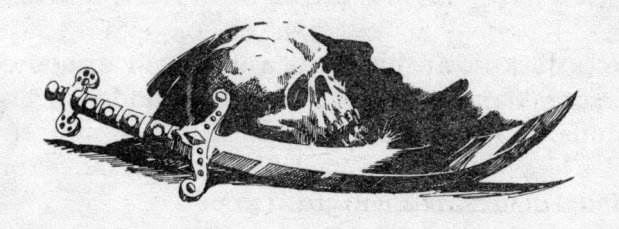

378

You trudge on, but find little dry ground. It is getting dark. The sun set in a blaze of fire a good fifteen minutes ago, and the swampy jungle is now cool and eerily quiet. You push aside great clumps of reeds, following the twisting path of dry ground, which seems to be leading you deeper and deeper into a maze. And then, although you were half expecting it . . . Turn to **372**.

379

You duck down hurriedly as a heavily armoured Lizard Man strides by. He stops suddenly, and sniffs the air for an almost unbearably long moment. Has he seen you – or smelt you? Then he moves on, and you breathe again. Turn to **32**.

380

Scurrying down conduits cut through the walls and then along trenches between the walls, you come to the built-up dockland area of the ruined outer city. This part of Vymorna has suffered less destruction than much of the besieged city, and seems not to be as heavily occupied by enemy troops. You creep up what used to be a gaily decorated alleyway between two roofless buildings, remembering with sadness the families who once lived here. The alley widens into a winding cobbled lane, which leads, via slopes and steps, down in the direction of the quayside. At that moment a shout comes from behind you. Two ragged Orcs, obviously scavenging among the ruins, race towards you. You have two simple options: will you stand and fight (turn to **365**) or run for it (turn to **234**)?

381

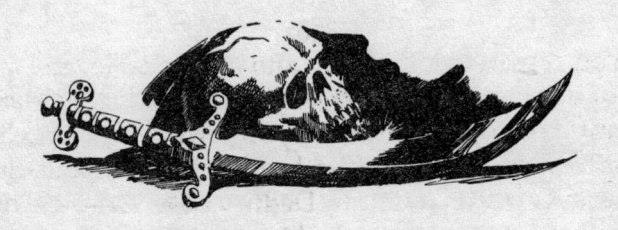

The warriors overcome you, pushing you to the ground so that they can bind you with tough vines. You are marched through the jungle until you come to a very large tree, whereupon a vine is attached to your waist and you are dragged up into the branches. Despite your initial shock at being so high above the ground, and the obvious danger of your predicament, you are intrigued by the platforms and rope-bridges that the warriors have built up in the tree-tops. A tall, white-haired elder, from his dress obviously the high priest or shaman, approaches you and stares deep into your eyes. If you have stared into another creature's eyes recently you will know of a paragraph to turn to. He takes your rucksack and shakes it out on to the floor and paws through the contents. Do you have a panther idol (turn to 308) or not (turn to 75)?

382

You slip in something red and unthinkable, and fall to your knees. A tall, heavily armoured Lizard Man, covered in gore, leaps at you, swinging a cruelly spiked war-flail at your head. You duck but the strands catch your arm. Deduct 1 STAMINA point, before you can return the blows.

LIZARD MAN   SKILL 8   STAMINA 6

If he scores two consecutive hits against you, turn to **162**. If you score two consecutive hits against him, or kill him, roll one die. If you roll 1–2, turn to **208**; 3–4, turn to **65**; 5–6, turn to **10**.

383

You hail the travellers, greeting them cordially. There is no reply; they sit motionless on their peculiar mounts, who regard you with their cold reptilian eyes. A chill breeze springs up and you give an involuntary shudder. 'What's the matter, friends? Have you lost your tongues?' you smile. Turn to **309**.

384

The messenger screams in panic, and then draws her sword and joins battle.

MESSENGER   SKILL 9   STAMINA 8

If you defeat her, turn to **103**.

385

The corridor slopes down, but, more peculiarly, twists in such a way that it angles sideways as well. It is very cool and dry down here, but also very musty, as though something once fresh has started to go off. You come to another room and peer in through the archway. This chamber is quite bizarre, for carved into all the available wall space are small niches. And standing in each niche is a skull and an ornate glass jar. Beneath each skull a metal plate is affixed to the wall. The skulls of ten thousand beings must be in here, you think, as you gaze in wonder. You peer closer at a niche, only to find that the skulls are not human at all. They are fluted, more as you imagine an Elf's skull to look, except that they also bear very exaggerated canine teeth! The jars next to each skull contain a nasty surprise for you, too, for each holds a small, wrinkled grey lump of flesh that might just be a brain! You can't make out what's written on the small metal plates – though there is definitely something there – for the symbols have become faded and illegible over the ages. This room is unsettling, especially for somewhere supposed to be a haven of Goodness. Two passages lead out of it: one flight of steps leads up to the left (turn to **182**) and another flight down to the right (turn to **4**).

386

Somehow you manage to stop yourself from falling. Most of the floor has gone, leaving a deep drop into the cellar beneath. You hide to one side of the doorway as an armoured Lizard Man strides past. Peering out after him, you are just in time to see him disappear among the ruins. There is no sign of the Marsh Orcs, thank Telak. Turn to **32**.

387

The Pterodactyl leaps skyward in a tremendous rush of wings, with you hanging on to its back. It soars high over the camp, and starts to head off towards the battlefield! The stupid reptile thinks it is going to fight! You grab its neck and try to steer it away from the battle, but all it does is go into a very steep dive, and you slip from its neck. As you fall through the air you have a moment to reflect on what a stupid move you have just made! Turn to **131**.

388

The pale liquid is a healing balm, which you may take when you need it most. When you wish to use its soothing powers make a note of the paragraph you are currently at, then turn to **42**. If you have another item to choose, turn to **31** (for the swirling globe) or turn to **13** (for the bow and arrows). If you now have your two items, turn to **361**.

389

'So you have met Lecarte, have you?' White-eye asks. 'Well, no, I traded this because it brought me bad luck, and I will not take it back.' Turn to **11** and choose again.

390

The enchanted arrow flies true and the Krell is pinned to the branch, dead. Seeing their friend's fate, the rest of the creatures leap screaming and chattering into the trees. You manage to retrieve your sword and belt, and buckle it back round your waist before moving on. Turn to **221**.

391

'I have news of this Laskar whom you seek,' says White-eye. 'I do not give freely, but I will gladly trade with you.' You cannot bring yourself to trade any of your father's things, but you may have something else to exchange. What can you trade?

Black lotus	Turn to **249**
Cloth o'gold	Turn to **49**
A mace	Turn to **129**
An Orc charm	Turn to **256**
A phial of purple liquid	Turn to **344**
Small panther idol	Turn to **389**

If you have nothing, or do not wish to trade, turn to **111**.

392

You bite into the body and almost choke. Dead Orc tastes absolutely terrible! You feel your stomach heave, but somehow you manage to keep from vomiting. Deduct 2 STAMINA points! 'And now, yoo young 'uns, 'tis time to meet yore elder relatives.' The younger Orcs line up to greet the more aged guests, and you seem expected to join them. Will you go along with them (turn to **287**), or try to make a break for it (turn to **66**)?

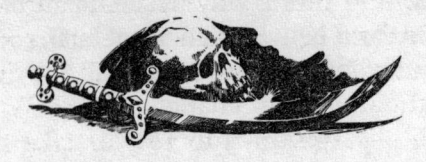

393

You haul yourself up a tree into the topmost branches, and from there you peer cautiously out over the jungle. It is a fabulous sight, like a green sea with the wind blowing it in waves. The forest rises up into the hills, less than a day's journey away. A pair of huge birds are flapping their way over the hills – eagles, perhaps. The south is covered in an evil yellow mist and your view is obscured, while the west is lost in a heat haze. To the north the jungle continues as far as the eye can see. Will you clamber down and continue your journey now (turn to **170**), or stay up here in the swaying branches a little longer (turn to **150**)?

394

You pull off the leaves near one end of the bundle, and give an involuntary shriek as a grinning skull leers out at you. It is a body, probably wrapped up in the leaves to preserve it, and crawling with maggots and spiders. Ugh, you shudder! Deduct 1 LUCK point, before climbing down and scrambling along the bridge. Turn to **199**.

395

The corridor curves gently upwards and leads to a small chamber, from which stone stairs spiral upwards; a narrow passage leads off to the right. That must be the way to the chapel of Telak. Will you go along the passage (turn to **165**) or take the stairs (turn to **301**)?

396

The messenger looks very relieved to have found another human on the road, and you notice she is very tired and dusty. She tells you her story – how she has been sent by the people of Coppertown far to the north to ask for aid against roving war-bands of Lizard Men and Mountain Trolls. Her face falls when you tell her of Vymorna's fate, and she appears devastated. You stand in silence for some minutes, before you dare make a move. Will you take her along with you (turn to **113**), or bid her farewell and set off again alone (turn to **103**)?

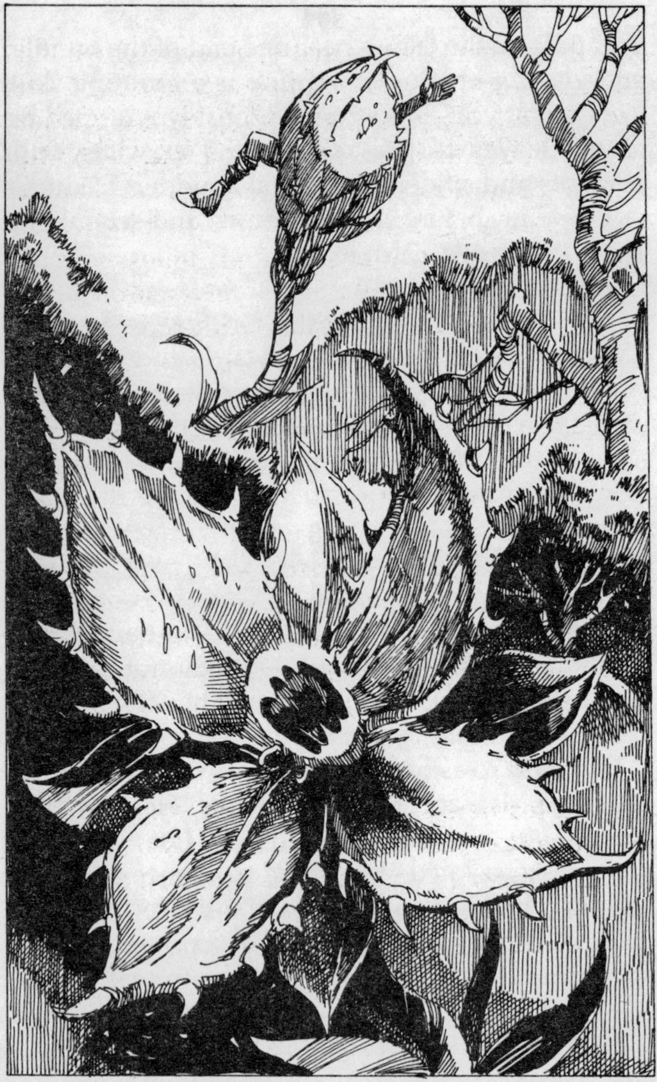

397

You know immediately that you have made a mistake as a huge fleshy jaw clamps tight around you. It belongs to a giant Venus Fly-Trap, and it has just caught you. Deduct 2 STAMINA points. You are now trapped inside the carnivorous plant, and all you can do is hack away at it with your knife. The plant will digest you in six rounds unless you can cut your way out. Roll one die for each of the six rounds and add the results of the die rolls together. If you score 20 or more points in six rounds the creature will die. If you score less than 20 points, it will digest you and your adventure will end here! If you cut yourself free from the plant, turn to **194**.

398

The hairs on your neck bristle and a chill shudder racks your body. Shapes loom and dance in the mist – big, bulky shapes. Will you turn and run back the way you came (turn to **195**) or stand your ground (turn to **39**)?

399

A black-feathered arrow thuds into your shoulder and you cry out in pain. Deduct 2 STAMINA points. If your STAMINA score is 6 or less, you lose your grip on the reins and fall from your riding lizard (turn to **114**). Otherwise you ride on (turn to **290**).

400

The blade cuts deep into the old man, slicing cleanly as the power guides your arm. The traitor dies, gurgling and choking. You step astride his body, the look in your eyes daring anyone to challenge you. The evil Lizard Men hesitate, unsure of just how much power you now have. You raise your sword aloft and in confirmation of your powers the air begins to shimmer. Coalescing from nothing, a thousand warriors materialize around you, golden weapons at the ready. The Lizard Men murmur in terror as the ancient soldiers begin to slice through their ranks. You turn away in disgust, but the sickening slaughter is soon over. With you at their head, the warriors step back into rank. You march away into the west, towards Vymorna, the power of your master, Telak Swordbearer, blazing through every atom of your body. With a force like this, charging into battle with the sun behind you, you will free Vymorna from the clutches of Evil and Chaos!